W9-AYY-860

PRO RATED LONGSHOTS:

A Proven Method for

Selecting Longshot Winners

PRO RATED LONGSHOTS:

A Proven Method for

Selecting Longshot Winners

DAN GEER

PARKER PUBLISHING COMPANY, INC.
WEST NYACK, N.Y.

© 1975 *by*

Parker Publishing Company, Inc.
West Nyack, N.Y.

All rights reserved. No part of this book may be reproduced in any form or by any means, without permission in writing from the publisher.

Library of Congress Cataloging in Publication Data

Geer, Dan,
   Pro rated longshots.

   1. Horse race betting. I. Title.
SF331.G43   798'.401   74-22369
ISBN 0-13-731554-6

Printed in the United States of America

In Memory of Henry Bomze,
Publisher of *American TURF Monthly*
and *Racing STAR Weekly*, for his unique
contributions to handicapping and
system play during the past 44 years

About This Book

Pro Rated Longshots is a new and powerful handicapping approach to high-priced winner-picking which is based on exhaustive study and research, over 20 years of statistics, and more than 50,000 winners paying 5 to 1 or more.

Once devised, *Pro Rated Longshots* was meticulously checked—*and proven*—throughout the entire year of 1972 at 24 leading tracks with spectacular results, averaging more than 100 winners per month.

All the payoffs exceeded $12, and almost half topped $20, with remarkable month-to-month consistency.

PRL is designed for veteran and novice racegoers alike. It is adaptable to either OTB (off-track betting) or to play at the track. It is readily understood and easy to apply.

Pro Rated Longshots is not based on the 1,001 tricky angles normally associated with longshot winner-picking. It does not depend on trainer moves, shifts in class, weight changes, jockey switches, distance switches, or recent claims. Nor is it connected with the many other factors used to pick winners at all prices. These include such things as:

> Class, form, consistency, money earned, speed ratings, final or fractional time, trainers, jockeys, breeding, weight, distance of race, track condition, age, sex, equipment carried, previous odds, and many, many more.

Horses are picked by simple, concise selection rules. These

encompass: 1. Preliminary Eliminations (including the Date Factor); 2. The Performance Rating; 3. The Price Factor. Play is on that horse qualifying on both the Date and Price Factors which has the highest Performance Rating.

The Basic Plan (pages 15-48) is completely mechanical: it tells you which horse to play, using minimum date rules, and leaves nothing to personal judgment. Examples of winners picked by the Basic Plan appear in Examples 1-10.

The Intermediate Plan (pages 49-64) shows you how to get additional winners by playing horses with more recent races than those required by the minimum date rules of the Basic Plan.

Picking these supplemental winners requires some personal judgment. You may be required to choose between two or more horses, or even to play two horses in the same race if the odds on them are sufficient. Examples of winners picked by the Intermediate Plan appear in Examples 11-13.

The Advanced Plan (pages 65-82) gives you further options, including Alternative Performance Ratings and Price Factors. It also shows you how to combine your own handicapping skill with the mechanical rules outlined in the Basic and Intermediate Plans. In this way, the Advanced Plan provides you with maximum flexibility in your search for high-priced payoffs

See Examples 14-15 for winners picked by two alternative approaches of the Advanced Plan.

It is essential that you learn each step separately before proceeding to the next one. Start by mastering the Basic Plan. Practice and re-practice its few, simple rules until you are letter-perfect in their application.

Many readers will wish to stop at this point and go no further. However, you may wish to examine the options available to you when playing horses with more-recent races. In this event, proceed to the Intermediate Plan.

And if you wish to explore still further variations of the

Basic Plan, perhaps even adding to it your own refinements, then turn to the Advanced Plan—but only after you have mastered all of the preceding material.

The decision should be yours. Only you can choose between a completely mechanical selection process at the one extreme and a completely flexible approach at the other.

Following the basic text are three appendices. Appendix 1 lists all winners picked by the Basic and Intermediate Plans for a complete year. Appendix 2 lists some additional winners for three months using an alternative Performance Rating of the Advanced Plan, and Appendix 3 some additional winners for three months with an alternative Price Factor.

There is also a Notes section where certain terms are defined and statistical data explained.

You are probably asking at this point whether *Pro Rated Longshots* can enable you to beat the races.

PRL is a tremendously effective high-price winner-picker. As you will see (on page 20) the Basic Plan beat five combined tracks for one full month *even assuming a play in every race.* This was done with completely mechanical rules and no supplementary eliminations or handicapping techniques.

If the Basic Plan can take you this far without personal judgment or last-minute refinements, just think what you can do with the options in the Intermediate and Advanced Plans plus your own racing know-how.

Whether you are a professional, regular, or neophyte, we sincerely believe that *PRL* is the most powerful and consistent longshot handicapping tool available today. It should make it far easier than you thought possible to stay ahead of the game.

Dan Geer

CONTENTS

PART 1

The Basic Plan

THE PROBLEM

"You must beat the prices to beat the races." We've all heard this a thousand times, and in theory it makes perfect sense— but it fails all too often in practice. Why? Primarily because we lack the confidence required to bet higher-priced horses against shorter-priced animals that everyone else seems to be backing.

Our 8-1 or 15-1 or 20-1 shot may look great on paper and he may be a tremendous overlay,[1]*but during the post parade we notice all the action that the favorite is getting and reluctantly conclude that the public choice must have some-thing going for it—otherwise all these people wouldn't be betting on it.

What happens, of course, is that we switch to the favorite and then watch in stupefied horror as our original play breezes home at astronomical odds.

It is the strain of playing losers—which is inevitable when betting higher-priced horses—that leads us to play shorter—and shorter-priced horses, until we wind up little better than "chalk players."[2]

Much the same pitfall awaits the handicapper who tries to weigh as many factors as possible before making his final

---

*The superior numbers (1-22) in the text refer to the Notes which begin on Page 83.

selection. By the time he figures out which is the classiest, fastest, and most formful horse in the race—with the best trainer and jockey—he, too, will wind up with the favorite, even though he reaches this point for reasons different from the frustrated longshot player's.

The net result is that most players substitute "winning percentage" for "overlays" when trying to beat the races—an approach which almost precludes their chances of doing so.

This narrow view of turf speculation ignores one essential part of the winning equation—the horse's odds today. It should be obvious that:

$$\text{Profit (or Loss)} = \text{Winning Percentage x Price}$$

Whether we cash one bet in ten at $20, two bets in ten at $10, or five bets in ten at even money we wind up with the same return.

However, in any series of ten plays, it is far easier to cash one winning ticket at $20 than five tickets at $4, because winning a race at *any* price is difficult when you consider the number of horses running against you and the many ways in which an animal can lose because of racing luck or other factors.

What's more, short prices—especially in the place and show slots—can double the effective takeout against you (assuming the take to be 15 percent) before you cash a nickel of your winning bet.[3]

Robert S. Dowst, in an article appearing in the February, 1973, issue of *American TURF Monthly*, shows that while the "actual" take on a $40 win ticket is about 15.8 percent, it reaches 20 percent on an $8 win payoff and 30 percent on a $4 win payoff.

That's not all. Breakage—the withholding of odd pennies above even payoff amounts such as $5.80, $5.60, or $5.40—increases geometrically with lower prices.[4]

In their almost frenzied striving to cash a ticket—at any price—racegoers overlook this vital stumbling block, thereby assuring ultimate failure. But they are not alone. One recent computer study—in attempting to isolate "winning factors"— has ignored the horse's price or odds today and devoted its entire attention to winning percentage.

The futility of this approach can best be shown by a simple example. Suppose that by your own handicapping, system play, or a rating method, you have "made" two horses which figure very close to each other.

Assume that your top-rated horse is quoted at 2-1 and your close-second-rated horse at 15-1. Too many of us, in this situation, will play the top-rated horse even though the second-rated horse is a far greater overlay.

Such a thing could never happen to the player who reads and follows the principles set forth in the next few pages.

THE SOLUTION: PRO RATED LONGSHOTS

In order to play high-priced overlays, the bettor must be convinced that they can win often enough to make backing them fun, and worthwhile. He must learn through experience that such horses can give him a real run for his money, and are not just hopeless longshots which only win through sheer luck or the "hatpin" method.

Pro Rated Longshots has been developed for this very purpose—to meet the need for that effective winning approach which concentrates not only on performance factors but also the essential ingredient of price.

After perusing its winning record for one full year, you should agree that many of the myths, prejudices, and fears which surround longshot play are without foundation. More importantly you will learn that it is almost as easy to win with higher-priced horses as with shorter-priced ones—and that long-shots win because of logical, not obscure, reasons.

What follows will provide you with a totally new perspective in your effort to beat the races.

WHAT IT IS

Pro Rated Longshots is a new handicapping approach to longshot winner-picking. It is designed to select horses, which through a combination of performance and price factors, give you a sufficient percentage edge or overlay to offset the ravages of take and breakage.

Despite its high average payoffs, *PRL* snags winners with almost ridiculous ease; many of its $20, $30, and $50 payoffs are obtained with no more effort than $5 or $10 winners with conventional selection methods.

PRL evolved from a 20-year study of more than 50,000 winners paying 5-1 or more. While the primary purpose of this research was to check $12 to $200 winners against existing systems, it became increasingly apparent that many high-priced winners had a common denominator not covered by these methods.

With further study, a new winning pattern gradually emerged which promised to be far more powerful than anything yet seen in the field of longshot handicapping.

In early 1972, it was decided to isolate this approach, refine it, and check it out at 24 leading major tracks for one full year. The net result exceeded all expectations.

POSITIVE PROOF OF PRL WIN POWER

Pro Rated Longshots during 1972 averaged more than 100 winners per month for the entire year. All its payoffs exceeded $12 and almost half topped $20. Its remarkable seasonal consistency can best be appreciated by the following table:

NUMBER OF WINNERS

Month	$12-$20	$20 and up	Total
January	57	55	113*
February	47	49	96

Month	$12-$20	$20 and up	Total
March	45	39	84
April	42	48	90
May	54	46	100
June	62	42	104
July	56	51	107
August	59	57	117*
September	42	50	94*
October	44	56	100
November	43	57	101*
December	57	55	112
Total:	608	605	1,218*

(*Totals include five ties for first place.)

This month-to-month record compares favorably with the percentage fluctuations of winning favorites at major tracks. For supposedly inconsistent longshots, it is little short of astounding.

Following is a further breakdown of all 1972 winners arranged in order of increasing payoffs:

$12-$20	$20-$30	$30-$50	$50-$100	$100 and up
608	326	181	81	17

The month-to-month consistency within these smaller groups was almost as marked as in the preceding table.

The 24 major tracks covered by our one-year study (in chronological order) were:

Liberty Bell, Bowie, Tropical Park, Gulfstream Park, Narragansett, Fair Grounds, Santa Anita, Aqueduct, Pimlico, Hialeah, Suffolk Downs, Garden State, Hawthorne, Belmont Park, Delaware Park, Arlington Park, Monmouth Park, Saratoga, Rockingham Park, Atlantic City, Sportsman's Park, Lincoln Downs, Laurel, and Calder Race Course.

With the exception of a few weeks at Lincoln Downs, when past performances were not available, our survey covered every day of every meeting during calendar year 1972.

During 1972, *PRL* was able to beat no fewer than 17 of

the 24 major tracks covered by our survey for at least one month.[5]

In September, 1972, its total payoffs at the five tracks in our survey—Belmont Park, Rockingham Park, Atlantic City, Sportsman's Park, and Lincoln Downs—exceeded the total amount that one would have bet with *one play in every race at each track for the entire month.* What's more, *PRL* does not average this many plays.

Finally, consider this comparison of *PRL* with two earlier systems devised by the same author.

The first, which we will call System "A", picks longshots; the second—System "B"—selects winners at all prices. However, the comparison is made only for winners paying $12 (5-1) or more.

Here is the breakdown of winners for the ten-month period from January 1 to October 31 of 1972. It covers all the tracks used in the survey of *Pro Rated Longshots.*

NUMBER OF WINNERS

	$12-$20	*$20-$30*	*$30-$50*	*$50-$100*	*$100-plus*	**Total*
System"A"	239	107	53	14	3	420
System "B"	397	133	71	34	1	640
PRL	508	267	143	69	14	1,005

*Totals include four ties (dead-heats) in each of three selection methods.

The above figures show that *PRL* clearly outperformed the other two selection methods in all price categories. And while it did not quite equal the combined total wins of the other two systems, it exceeded them in all except the lowest payoff range.[6] What's more, its proportion of winners increased geometrically with each higher payoff range, reaching a ratio of almost 5-1 in the $100-plus category.

Since Systems "A" and "B" are established selection metnods—having been featured both in *Sports Illustrated* and

The New York Times—this comparison should give you some idea of the winning power of *Pro Rated Longshots.*

Some Spectacular Winners

Having shown you some general accomplishments of *Pro Rated Longshots* let's look at a few of its high-priced winners.[7]

Perhaps a good starting point is the 1972 Preakness at Pimlico—one of the famed Triple Crown events.

As you probably remember, Riva Ridge was a top-heavy favorite going into this race, having won the Kentucky Derby. Several other horses were heavily backed in the betting. But when the race had been run, the winner was a rank outsider— Bee Bee Bee—who paid $39.40.

Bee Bee Bee was a Pro Rated Longshot, and a real standout selection of the *PRL.* Just how good a play, will become apparent in the section on example races.

While this was a notable achievement, it can not compare pricewise with these winners picked by *Pro Rated Longshots* in the first and second races at Gulfstream Park, January 26, 1972:

NOBLE DUEL $230.40
SY'S THEME $119.60

The daily double payoff on these two top-rated selections amounted to $6,683.60—a record high for Gulfstream Park!

Another historic win for the PRL occurred at Lincoln Downs on September 28 when it picked this winner in the first race:

PAWN $187.60

This payoff was the first half of the biggest daily double in the history of North American racing—a stupendous $15,005.00 return on a $2 ticket! The winner of the second race, which did not qualify as a selection of the *PRL,* paid only $46. Although only two tickets were sold on this winning combination, bettors who had wheeled Pawn with the 12 horses in the second race (by buying 12 separate daily double combinations) could have received the equivalent of a $1,250 return on a $2 ticket.

On February 23 at Bowie, *PRL* snagged these Pro Rated Longshots in the 5th, 7th, and 8th races:

```
CRIMSONADE  . . . . . . . . . . . $25.40
JACK THE SAILOR . . . . . . . . . $56.60
SON O'FANCY  . . . . . . . . . . . $18.40
```

There were four winners paying $20 or more at Lincoln Downs on October 14 (the others paid less than $12) and PRL had every one of them. The winners were:

```
FLYING JORAYME . . . . . . . . . $35.00
CONTOS . . . . . . . . . . . . . . $22.20
LINDEN CREEK  . . . : . . . . . . $20.20
DAD DAW . . . . . . . . . . . . . $21.80
```

Players who had relied on luck or other arbitrary means would have had one chance in 15,000 of hitting these four top-rated *PRL* selections!

Just five horses were entered in the third race at Belmont Park on September 21 and they went postward at 11-1, 26-1, 2-1, 3-2, and 8-5, respectively. The only horse in this field qualifying as a Pro Rated Longshot was Opinionation—the extreme outsider—whose winning payoff came to $55.80.

On September 5, in the fifth race at the same track, Coraggioso was the only qualified *PRL* selection in a nine-horse field. As the second highest choice in the betting, she returned $81.00 to win.

PRL caught these bombshells at different tracks on the same day (May 18). The two winners were:

```
Suf    TARTAN JOHN  . . . . . . $108.20
Haw    LINDEN WAY  . . . . . . . $180.40
```

These top-rated *PRL* selections were exact opposites in the range of *Pro Rated Longshot* ratings, the winner at Suffolk Downs having a very high point score, and the Hawthorne selection earning a very low one. (The latter horse qualified because there were no other plays in the same race.)

This flexibility in selection-making is one of the chief advantages of *PRL*.

The winners we have listed so far—all of which were picked by the Basic Play of *PRL* and entailed playing only one horse in a race—might be considered fluke happenings were they not supported by the overwhelming weight of other daily doubles, two-, three- and four-winner days, and blockbuster single payoffs which took place almost steadily throughout the entire year 1972.

To summarize what *Pro Rated Longshots* has done and is continuing to do:

It has exploded the myths that:

- Longshot winners cannot be picked consistently.
- Winning longshots depend on obscure, tricky angles and/or trainer moves.
- It is impossible to beat the races when betting more than one or two races per day.

It has proved that:

- You must get a worthwhile price on your winners to offset the effect of take and breakage.
- It is often nearly as easy to secure a high-priced winner as a lower-priced one.

HOW IT WORKS

PRL is based, very simply, on *running positions* (including finishing positions), or more specifically, the horse's running positions in its three most recent races.

Pro Rated Longshots seeks horses which were running

first, second, or third in as many calls[8] as possible of their top three races.

As you will see, when studying the selection process, we consider four calls or stages in the horse's top three races, and its Performance Rating is based on the number of points it can earn by running forwardly[9] (1, 2, 3) at these various calls.

You might ask at this point how we can afford to concentrate solely on running positions and ignore the many other factors used to judge a horse's current capabilities.

The answer is that running positions—including the finish—are the end result of all other factors (such as class, form, speed, consistency, breeding, etc.). A horse cannot be leading, or running close to the leader, at any stage of a race (including the finish) unless it has the current form, inherent class, and speed to cope with its field.

These other factors and angles, important as they may be, are reflected in running positions and finishing positions in a horse's most recent races.

You might also think that a horse running 1, 2, or 3 in as many calls as possible has to fit one of the following patterns:

1. Front-runner.

2. Early-speed horse.

3. In-the-money finisher.

While a Pro Rated Longshot often falls into one or more of these categories, it is not required to do so. Many horses, especially those with lower Performance Ratings, do not answer any such description.

The Performance Rating is so flexible that a horse can run any pattern (including an "even race" or "come-from-behind" effort) and still qualify as the top-rated *PRL* selection in its field.

WHY IT WORKS

Having explained the general theory of *how* it works, by describing the nub of the selection process, we will now show you *why* it works—i.e., why it is able to secure so many winners at out-of-line prices.

The answer is that a horse, in order to qualify, must have finished out of the money in its last race, thereby increasing the liklihood of its going postward at attractive odds today.

There is probably no single factor which enhances a horse's post-time odds like an out-of-the-money finish in its last race. The betting public is all too prone to judge a horse's chances by this one call—ignoring all the other calls—so that its odds primarily depend on whether it finished in or out of the money in its most recent race.

The following diagrams, which show a horse's running positions at the calls of its top three races, should make this point absolutely clear and explain why *PRL* is able to command such high-priced payoffs.

Underlay Pattern   **Overlay Pattern**

5	6	5	(1)		1	2	3	(5)
8	9	6	5		2	2	2	3
8	4	5	6		1	1	2	2

The left-hand diagram shows a horse which is almost sure to be overbet today. This classic underlay situation stems from the fact that the horse won its last race but showed absolutely nothing at the other 11 calls of its top three races. The public, as usual, looks only at the finish of the top race and practically ignores the other calls.

(The effect would be much the same if the horse had finished second or third in its top race. Often the only way for its trainer to get a price on his horse is to move it up sharply in class.)

The right-hand diagram, by way of contrast, shows a classic overlay pattern. Here the horse finished out of the money in its last race but was running first, second, or third at every other call in its top three races. The betting public again will miss the boat, overlooking the horse because of its most recent finishing position while ignoring the other calls.

While these are two extreme cases, the overlay pattern shown in the right-hand diagram is what gives *Pro Rated Longshots* its tremendous percentage edge. Since only one call (finish of top race) is required to enhance the horse's odds, this leaves 11 calls to provide ample evidence of the horse's winning capability in today's race.

The very fact that 11 calls are required to arrive at the horse's Performance Rating, which in turn determines its winning capability, explains the winning power and flexibility of *PRL*.

It might almost be called a composite of 11 different systems, since many selection methods have been structured on only one or two specific calls. For example:

1. Horse showed early speed (i.e., ran 1, 2, or 3) at the first call of its top race.

2. Horse finished in the money in its next-to-last race.

3. Horse was 1, 2, or 3 at the pre-stretch call in its third race back, or bottom race.

All of these betting angles are able to secure occasional longshot winners but since they are restricted to specific calls they can not win consistently. A horse might win one race with Angle 1 but lose the next race to an animal which qualified on Angle 2. Subsequent races might be won by horses qualifying on still other angles, and so on.

Pro Rated Longshots weighs all of these potential systems—each of which is based on one specific call—and chooses the horse most likely to win only after all of the calls have been compared and evaluated for each horse in today's race.

The fact that a horse is not required to qualify on any one call, but on the sum total of 11 different calls, explains the flexibility of *PRL,* and this flexibility in turn explains the remarkable consistency of its high-priced winners.

We are now ready to examine the selection process.

THE SELECTION PROCESS

PRL selects its plays in three steps:

Preliminary Eliminations (including the Date Factor)

The Performance Rating

The Price Factor

We will now consider these steps in greater detail.

Preliminary Eliminations

Before applying the Performance Rating, eliminate those horses which:

1. Finished first, second, or third in their last race.
   a. Consider the original finishing position only; ignore disqualifications (moving the horse higher or lower, or disqualifications from purse money).10
   b. Horses which tie or dead-heat for third are considered to have finished third.

2. Have fewer than three races in their racing careers, as shown by their past-performance records.

3. Do not meet the following Date Factor requirements:
   a. Last race within 30 days, next-to-last race within 60 days, third race back within 90 days.
   b. Maximum interval of 60 days between two successive races in the three-race span.

Rule 2 eliminates all first-time starters and horses which have raced only once or twice in their lifetimes. Rule 3b limits to 60 days the interval between the last and next-to-last race, and between the next-to-last and third race back.

Having reduced the field to horses which ran out of the money last start, show at least three races in their past performances, and meet the minimum date rules, we are ready for the next step.

The Performance Rating

As you now know, *PRL* is based on running positions in the running lines[11] of the horse's three most recent races.

It is essential at this point to distinguish between running positions and beaten lengths. In the sample running lines below, running positions are shown by the superior or big numbers and the beaten lengths by the inferior or small numbers.

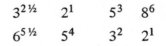

$$3^{2\frac{1}{2}} \quad 2^1 \quad 5^3 \quad 8^6$$
$$6^{5\frac{1}{2}} \quad 5^4 \quad 3^2 \quad 2^1$$

Running positions, in most editions of the *Daily Racing Form,* are shown at four calls of each race. But in the Eastern *Racing Form* (formerly *The Morning Telegraph*) five calls are included.[12] When using the Eastern Edition of the *Daily Racing Form,* ignore the left-hand call (which appears immediately after the post position) and use only the four right-hand calls.

These calls are known as:

1. First call.

2. Pre-stretch (or second) call.

3. In-stretch (or stretch) call.

4. Finish.

As mentioned above we consider running positions in the three most recent races (paying no attention to beaten-length margins).

Since the most recent race appears on the top line of the horse's past-performance record, the next-to-last race on the second line, and the race before that on the third line down, we will refer to these races as follows:

Most recent   —Top Race

Next-to-last   —Middle Race

Third race back   —Bottom Race

The calls used to rate a horse are shown in the following diagram exactly as they appear in the horse's past performances:

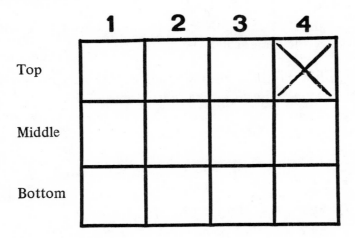

As we have already required the horse to finish out of the money in its top race, this call is not considered in the rating score. We have therefore crossed it out in the diagram shown above.

Using the 11 remaining calls in the diagram we rate each qualified horse (after preliminary eliminations) as follows:

1. It receives 3 points each time it was running (or finished) *first* at one of the 11 calls.
2. It receives 2 points each time it was running (or finished) *second* at one of the 11 calls.
3. It receives 1 point each time it was running (or finished) *third* at one of the 11 calls.

While the final calls (Call 4) in the middle and bottom races are finishing rather than running positions, they are scored in exactly the same way. However, there are two exceptions:

1. A horse can finish in a tie (dead-heat) for first, second, or third at the finish or final call, but ties are not shown for running positions at earlier calls.
2. Disqualifications apply only to the finish or final call, not to the earlier calls.

Disqualifications, as already pointed out, are completely ignored. Rate the horse according to its original finish.

In the event that the horse finished in a dead-heat for win, place, or show in its middle or bottom race, such ties are rated as follows:

1. Tie for first   −2½ points.
2. Tie for second −1½ points.
3. Tie for third   −½ point.

Now let's return to our diagram. As 11 calls are considered

in rating the horse, and since it can receive 1, 2, or 3 points at each call, its Performance Rating can range from 1 (minimum) to 33 (maximum) points. It must receive at least 1 point to qualify.

Exception: Where the horse finished in a tie (dead-heat) for third in either its middle or bottom race, and was not running either first, second, or third at any other call, it can qualify with only 1/2 point.

To be sure you understand how to apply the Performance Ratings, figure out the point scores in the following examples:

Horse A   **Horse B**

2	2	3	~~5~~
8	6	1	2
3	2	3	8

8	6	3	~~5~~
1	1	3	5
8	6	5	8

Horse A gets a Performance Rating of 14 points; Horse B, a rating of 8 points.

To double check yourself, first figure the successive totals reading from left to right, top line to bottom line; then total the firsts, seconds, and thirds (multiplied by 3, 2, and 1). The two totals should agree.

This completes the Performance Rating. After preliminary eliminations each remaining horse should have received a rating score ranging from 1 to 33 points.

The Price Factor

The fact that a horse finished out of the money in its top

race, as just pointed out, should enhance its odds today, but to insure worthwhile odds on our selections we stipulate that:

Every horse which has received a Performance Rating must also meet these minimum odds requirements:

1. Its closing toteboard odds must be at least 5-1.
2. Its morning line odds must also be at least 5-1, using one, but not both, of the following:
   a. Competent public selector (such as Sweep or Hermis) in the *Daily Racing Form* or any good daily newspaper.
   b. Morning line in track program (compiled by the track handicapper) which also appears as the first set of odds on the toteboard.

For on-track play it is recommended that you use:

1. Latest possible toteboard odds.
2. Morning line in track program.

The track program is preferable to the morning line of public selectors because it includes all scratches except late scratches.

For off-track play (OTB) we suggest that you use:

1. Scratch sheet (such as Armstrong's).
2. Morning line of public selector.

The scratch sheet has the most accurate line available, short of toteboard odds, and it, too, includes all except late scratches. It is, therefore, recommended as the best substitute for last-minute tote odds. And since the track program is not available for off-track play, you should turn to the next best thing—the morning line of a competent public selector such as Sweep, Hermis or Handicap.

Note: If the scratch sheet is not available in your area and you are playing off track, then use the morning line odds of a public sector only.

After eliminating those horses which are less than 5-1 on the first Price Factor (toteboard odds/scratch sheet) or the second Price Factor (track program/public selector's morning line), we will wind up, in the average race, with one to five horses receiving Performance Ratings.[13]

Making The Final Selection

We are now ready to make our final selection. Before going further, let's review the steps we have followed so far.

The horse or horses being considered for play:

1. Have run out of the money in their top race.
2. Show at least three races in their past performances.
3. Meet the minimum date requirements.
4. Have a Performance Rating of at least 1 point.
5. Have closing (last-minute) toteboard odds of at least 5-1 (or scratch sheet odds of at least 5-1 for off-track play).
6. Are also at least 5-1 on the track program (or morning line of competent public selector for off-track play).

Your play is the highest-rated horse meeting all of the above qualifications.

To be sure you understand this procedure, let's consider the following hypothetical example:

Horse	Points	Closing Tote Odds	Morning Line Odds
A	5	10-1	8-1
B	8	8-1	12-1
C	15	5-1	3-1

The top-rated horse in this example is Horse C, but since it is only 3-1 on the morning line it is eliminated by the Price Factor. Horse C would also be eliminated if its closing odds were 3-1 and its morning line odds 5-1, or both odds were 3-1.

Of the remaining horses, both of which qualify on the first Price Factor (minimum toteboard odds) and the Second Price Factor (minimum morning line odds), we choose Horse B, the one with the higher Performance Rating.

Now let's look at some example races so you can see exactly how to pick *Pro Rated Longshots* winners.

Examples 1-10 show how top-rated horses, which qualify on the minimum date and odds rules, were picked by *PRL*.

EXAMPLE RACES

Some Pro Rated Longshots are just screaming to be played. Here is the almost perfect example:

Example 1
September 21, 1972—Belmont Park 3

In this 2-year-old allowance race for non-winners of races other than maiden or claiming, only five horses are entered after scratches.

They are listed in post position order, together with all the information needed to make your *PRL* selections.

Horse	Dates of Top Three Races	Running Positions	Morning Line Odds	Post Time Odds $1
Chuka Drummer	9 Sept 72	6 7 7 5	8-1	11.00
	23 Aug 72	6 5 3 1		

Horse	Dates of Top Three Races	Running Positions	Morning Line Odds	Post Time Odds $1
Opinionation	9 Sept 72	3 4 5 7	12-1	26.90
	19 Aug 72	2 3 4 8		
	9 Aug 72	2 1 1 1		
Trevose	9 Sept 72	5 2 2 2	4-1	2.30
	2 Sept 72	6 6 3 3		
	26 Aug 72	6 7 7 8		
Propellent	25 Aug 72	1 1 1 1	2-1	1.50
	17 Aug 72	7 6 4 3		
	7 Aug 72	7 7 5 3		
Broadway Playboy	13 Sept 72	1 2 1 2	5-2	1.60
	7 Aug 72	11 9 9 9		

In this race, all the horses except Opinionation are eliminated by the Preliminary Elimination Rules: Chuka Drummer,
because he has only two races in his past performance record;
Trevose and Propellent, because they finished in the money in
their top race; Broadway Playboy because he has fewer than
three races and also finished second in his top race. (The latter
three horses are also eliminated because they are less than 5-1
both on the morning line and post-time odds).

Opinionation has finished out of the money in his top
race, has at least three races, and meets the minimum date
requirements. His Performance Rating is 15 points, and he is 5-1
or higher both on the morning line (Hermis in the Eastern
Racing Form) and closing toteboard odds.

Opinionation, a standout *PRL* selection on all counts,
returned a win payoff of $55.80.

Example 2
September 29, 1972—Atlantic City 8

In this 3-year-old allowance race there are seven horses
entered after scratches.

Horse	Dates of Top Three Races		Running Positions				Morning Line Odds	Post Time Odds $1
Mongo's Image	21 Sept 72		2	4	5	8	12-1	26.20
	13 Sept 72		2	3	4	7		
	23 Aug 72		3	2	1	1		
I'm Ed	8 July 72		1	1	1	1	5-1	9.20
	17 June 72		2	1	1	2		
	7 June 72		7	9	10	10		
Barely Once	16 Sept 72		6	7	7	5	2-1	3.20
	3 July 72		1	1	1	1		
	6 June 72		3	2	1	1		
Golden Crock	21 Sept 72		4	3	2	3	8-1	6.60
	23 Aug 72		1	1	2	5		
	12 July 72		4	2	1	1		
Dundas Prince	22 Sept 72		3	1	1	1	5-2	1.20
	15 Sept 72		4	4	4	6		
	17 Aug 72		3	2	2	2		
Duc by Right	26 Aug 72		7	6	7	7	10-1	4.10
	19 July 72		5	6	4	5		
	1 July 72		5	5	3	1		
Red Bayou	22 Sept 72		6	6	6	6	8-1	13.00
	23 Aug 72		3	3	3	3		
	5 Aug 72		1	1	3	4		

Now let's take the selection steps in order.

Preliminary Eliminations—Mongo's Image, OK; I'm Ed eliminated because of finishing in money in top race and not meeting minimum date requirements. Barely Once eliminated by date requirements (more than 60 days since middle race, more than 90 days since bottom race, more than 60 days between top and middle races). Golden Crock and Dundas Prince eliminated because they finished in money in their top race. Duc by Right eliminated by minimum date requirement— more than 30 days since last race. Red Bayou is OK.

Performance Ratings—Mongo's Image gets 14 points, Red Bayou gets 11 points.

Price Factor—Both horses are 5-1 or higher on morning line and post-time odds.

Final selection is Mongo's Image who returned $54.40 to win.

Example 3
September 12, 1972–Rockingham Park 2

There are ten horses entered in this $2,500 claimer.

Horse	Dates of Top Three Races	Running Positions				Morning Line Odds	Post Time Odds $1
La Z Boy	4 Sept 72	1	1	1	1	4-1	12.10
	17 Aug 72	5	5	7	6		
	10 Aug 72	8	7	7	5		
Ata Blue	4 Sept 72	9	9	9	9	20-1	42.30
	26 Aug 72	6	8	8	8		
	19 Aug 72	7	6	6	6		
Sister's Dojo	1 Sept 72	5	5	5	5	10-1	13.20
	22 Aug 72	9	9	10	10		
	1 Aug 72	4	3	4	4		
Plain Or Fancy	1 Sept 72	7	7	7	7	6-1	21.20
	14 June 72	9	9	9	8		
	7 June 72	6	6	5	2		
Sid's Girl	24 Aug 72	7	5	5	5	10-1	12.60
	14 Aug 72	8	8	8	8		
	7 Aug 72	4	7	6	4		
Sentient	1 Sept 72	4	6	6	6	20-1	37.80
	22 Aug 72	7	10	11	11		
	1 Aug 72	5	5	3	3		
Missile Ladd	1 Sept 72	6	4	3	2	5-2	1.60
	22 Aug 72	6	5	3	3		
	16 Aug 72	11	11	11	11		
Riot Control	1 Sept 72	3	2	2	3	3-1	3.30
	22 Aug 72	2	1	2	4		
	11 Aug 72	5	9	10	10		
Pump Nut	29 Aug 72	7	7	7	7	20-1	19.30
	22 Aug 72	8	8	8	8		
	9 Aug 72	7	7	7	7		
Halatose	7 Sept 72	1	2	4	5	20-1	3.60
	1 Sept 72	2	3	4	4		
	22 Aug 72	5	6	7	6		

Preliminary Eliminations—La Z Boy, Missile Ladd, and Riot Control are eliminated because they finished in the money in their top races. Plain Or Fancy is eliminated by the minimum date rules.

Performance Ratings—Ata Blue gets no points; Sister's Dojo, 1 point; Sid's Girl, no points; Sentient, 2 points; Pump Nut, no points; Halatose, 8 points. Sister's Dojo, Sentient, and Halatose qualify.

Price Factor—Halatose is eliminated because post-time odds are less than 5-1. Sister's Dojo and Sentient are at least 5-1 both on morning line and closing tote odds. Sentient (2 points) is the play.

Sentient won and paid $77.60.

This race shows how a horse with a low Performance Rating can still qualify as a final *PRL* selection. Also note how horses with in-the-money finishes went off at short prices. Finally, the wisdom of having two minimum price requirements was dramatically borne out by Halatose (20-1 on morning line) being bet down to only 7-2. The morning line alone would not have eliminated this horse from play.

Example 4
May 20, 1972—Pimlico 8 (The Preakness)

The following horses were entered in this race (after scratches). Running lines have been omitted for those finishing in the money in their top race.

Horse	Dates of Top Three Races	Running Positions				Morning Line Odds	Post Time Odds $1
No Le Hace					2	5-1	5.70
Riva Ridge					1	4-5	.30
Key To The Mint					1	5-2	4.20
Eager Exchange	22 Apr 72	6	7	9	9	12-1	47.50
	8 Apr 72	3	1	1	2		
	1 Apr 72	8	6	6	11		

Horse	Dates of Top Three Races	Running Positions				Morning Line Odds	Post Time Odds $1
Hassi's Image	6 May 72	4	6	9	11	30-1	59.10
	22 Apr 72	5	6	6	6		
	14 Apr 72	5	4	4	4		
Festive Mood	6 May 72	10	7	5	4	30-1	65.60
	22 Apr 72	8	10	6	7		
	8 Apr 72	9	11	10	11		
Bee Bee Bee	6 May 72	2	2	2	5	7-1	18.70
	29 Apr 72	3	3	1	1		
	21 Apr 72	1	1	1	1		

Preliminary Eliminations—No Le Hace, Riva Ridge, and Key To The Mint are eliminated because they finished in the money in their top race. (The latter two horses would also have been eliminated by the Price Factor).

Performance Ratings—Eager Exchange gets 9 points; Hassi's Image, no points; Festive Mood, no points; Bee Bee Bee, 26 points. Only Eager Exchange and Bee Bee Bee qualify.

Price Factor—Both horses are OK on the price rule so Bee Bee Bee is the final selection.

Bee Bee Bee, a standout selection with a very high Performance Rating, beat the heavily favored Riva Ridge (and Key To The Mint), returning $39.40.

Example 5
January 26, 1972—Gulfstream Park 1

Twelve horses were entered in this race, a $5,000 claimer.

Horse	Rates of Top Three Races	Running Positions				Morning Line Odds	Post Time Odds $1
French Steak	3 Jan 72	11	11	10	9	4-1	4.20
	20 Dec 71	7	7	7	7		
	7 Dec 71	4	4	5	5		

Horse	Rates of Top Three Races	Running Positions				Morning Lines Odds	Post Time Odds $1
Strongman	11 Dec 71	12	12	12	11	30-1	35.10
	9 Oct 71	7	7	4	3		
	2 Oct 71	2	4	6	7		
Makinroy					2	12-1	5.80
Madam Mim					2	12-1	39.90
Wopeedah	7 Dec 71	5	5	6	4	6-1	7.50
	30 Nov 71	8	8	6	5		
	23 Nov 71	6	4	4	3		
Octory					2	10-1	10.90
Small Target					2	3-1	2.10
Bokir	First-time starter					10-1	22.90
Meadows Hope					2	8-1	11.30
Margie C.	3 Jan 72	6	8	7	6	8-1	9.30
	27 Dec 71	3	1	1	2		
	10 Dec 71	2	1	2	2		
Noble Duel	8 Jan 72	2	10	10	10	30-1	114.20
	21 Dec 71	2	2	1	1		
	10 Dec 71	2	2	1	3		
Arcadia Kid	13 Jan 72	9	9	6	6	15-1	12.60
	30 Dec 71	11	10	12	12		
	18 Nov 71	3	3	1	1		

Preliminary Eliminations—Makinroy, Madam Mim, Octory, Small Target, and Meadows Hope are eliminated because they finished second in their top race. (Small Target also failed to meet the minimum date rule.) Strongman and Wopeedah failed to meet the minimum date requirement. Bokir is eliminated because he has no races.

Performance Ratings—French Steak gets no points; Margie C., 18 points; Noble Duel, 20 points; Arcadia Kid, 8 points. Only the last three horses qualify.

Price Factor—All three horses are all right on morning line and post-time odds.

Final selection is Noble Duel who returned an astounding $230.40 to win, after romping by six lengths. The comment on this horse, who went off at nearly three times the odds of any other horse in the race, was: "Hardly the one." Reigh Count had him at the bottom of his morning line.

Example 6
January 26, 1972–Gulfstream Park 2

Again we have a full field of 12 starters in this $7,500 claimer.

Horse	Dates of Top Three Races	Running Positions				Morning Line Odds	Post Time Odds $1
Aqua Stitch	14 Jan 72	1	1	2	8	12-1	4.80
	6 Jan 72	1	1	1	1		
	11 Nov 71	1	1	1	2		
I Will Do It	7 Jan 72	6	6	6	7	5-1	15.80
	17 Dec 71	4	8	10	10		
	6 Dec 71	8	8	8	7		
Unto Heaven	27 Oct 71	6	9	9	9	8-1	3.30
	19 Oct 71	1	2	6	7		
	17 Sept 71	2	4	8	8		
Keydunfee	24 Dec 71	9	7	6	8	3-1	4.70
	6 Dec 71	7	5	4	5		
	2 Dec 71	8	4	3	1		
Lady Carmella	26 Nov 71	7	7	7	7	30-1	26.00
	10 Nov 71	10	10	11	8		
	29 Oct 71	8	6	5	4		
Hy's Tracie					2	30-1	23.60
Forgive Divine	15 Jan 72	6	7	7	7	12-1	24.90
	1 Jan 72	9	6	4	3		
	22 Dec 71	8	5	4	4		
Iron Tonette					1	5-1	9.10
Gentle Times	12 Jan 72	7	7	6	5	30-1	23.80
	5 Jan 72	8	8	8	8		
	29 Dec 71	6	5	7	7		

Horse	Dates of Top Three Races	Post Time Odds $1				Morning Line Odds	Post Time Odds $1
Real Tharp	15 Jan 72	10	9	8	8	12-1	30.70
	6 Jan 72	9	6	4	2		
	28 Dec 71	11	8	6	5		
Two Hopes	15 Jan 72	8	8	7	6	6-1	2.70
	7 Jan 72	5	4	3	4		
	31 Dec 71	3	3	2	3		
Sy's Theme	27 Dec 71	4	5	8	9	15-1	58.80
	13 Dec 71	1	2	3	4		
	8 Dec 71	6	6	5	5		

Preliminary Eliminations—Hy's Tracie and Iron Tonette are eliminated because they finished in the money in their top race; Unto Heaven, Keydunfee, and Lady Carmella by the minimum date rules.

Performance Ratings—Aqua Stitch gets 31 points; I Will Do It, no points; Forgive Divine, 1 point; Gentle Times, no points; Real Tharp, 2 points; Two Hopes, 6 points; Sy's Theme, 6 points.

Price Factor—Aqua Stitch is eliminated because her closing odds are only 4.80 to 1. Two Hopes is eliminated because his post-time odds are also less than 5-1 (2.70).

Of the other four horses, Sy's Theme has the greatest number of points and, therefore, is the final selection. Her win payoff was $119.60. The daily double payoff on these two winning *PRL* selections was $6,683.60! Only 17 $2 tickets were sold on this record-breaking double at Gulfstream Park which topped the previous record by almost $2,000.

Example 7
September 5, 1972—Belmont Park 5

There are nine horses in this allowance race for 2-year-old fillies.

Horse	Dates of Top Three Races	Running Positions	Morning Line Odds	Post Time Odds $1
Gypsy Blade		3	6-1	4.40^e

Horse	Dates of Top Three Races		Running Positions				Morning Lines Odds	Post Time Odds $1
Sweet Sop						3	4-1	5.30
Coraggioso	12 Aug 72	11	10	10	11		8-1	39.50
	19 Jul 72	3	2	1	1			
	1 Jul 72	4	5	5	4			
Kelstone						1	10-1	12.30
Desoto Belle						3	15-1	32.10
Petty Thievery						1	3-1	2.50
Jimminy Gosh	25 Aug 72	2	2	10	10		6-1	4.40[e]
	11 Aug 72	1	1	1	1			
	28 Jul 72	2	2	1	1			
Tuerta						1	5-2	1.30
Bo Alison						1	10-1	40.80

Preliminary Eliminations—Gypsy Blade, Sweet Sop, Kelstone, Desoto Belle, Petty Thievery, Tuerta, and Bo Alison finished in the money in their top race.

Performance Ratings—Coraggioso gets 9 points; Jimminy Gosh, 26 points.

Price Factor—Jimminy Gosh, coupled with Gypsy Blade as part of an entry in the betting (shown by letter "e" after the odds), has closing odds below 5-1

This leaves Coraggioso, with 9 points, as the only qualified play. This filly paid $81.00 to win.

Another perfect example of how so many *PRL* standouts are picked by exclusion rather than comparative ratings. Not every race is this easy but this sort of opportunity occurs most often in 2-year-old and maiden races.

Example 8
March 30, 1972—Hialeah 5

There are 12 horses in this $6,250 claimer for 3-year-old fillies.

Horse	Dates of Top Three Races		Running Positions				Morning Lines Odds	Post Time Odds $1
Missy Michelle	20 Mar 72	2	2	4	9		20-1	33.40
	8 Nov 71	9	9	9	9			
	11 Oct 71	1	2	7	8			
Tupalou	21 Mar 72	3	5	12	12		5-1	68.00
	1 Mar 72	7	10	11	11			
	17 Feb 72	2	1	1	2			
Delso	24 Mar 72	8	7	4	4		3-1	1.80
	13 Mar 72	2	3	1	1			
	1 Feb 72	5	7	8	7			
My Sense	7 Jan 72	2	3	3	5		8-1	22.50
	30 Dec 71	3	2	2	4			
	20 Dec 71	1	2	3	8			
Royal Care	21 Mar 72	6	6	3	7		4-1	5.20
	9 Mar 72	1	1	1	1			
	15 Jan 72	6	7	11	10			
Come to the	23 Feb 72	6	7	7	8		30-1	198.20
	9 Feb 72	9	10	8	9			
	12 Jan 72	10	10	10	8			
Decathagal	10 Mar 72	5	11	12	12		20-1	122.80
	21 Feb 72	6	10	11	11			
	9 Feb 72	9	12	Eased				
Bamboo	21 Mar 72	7	10	10	8		20-1	15.70
	6 Mar 72	7	8	8	7			
	15 Feb 72	6	11	12	12			
S. D. Delight	13 Mar 72	1	1	3	4		4-1	5.90
	1 Mar 72	3	3	3	8			
	17 Feb 72	3	5	12 E'd				
Shergaul						1	5-1	4.20
Nearly Mine						1	10-1	23.30
Hope Child	1 Feb 72	3	4	7	9		12-1	5.30
	6 Jan 72	5	5	5	5			
	13 Dec 71	4	3	2	1			

Preliminary Eliminations—Shergaul and Nearly Mine finished in the money in their top race. Missy Michelle, My Sense, Come to the Ball, and Hope Child fail to meet the minimum date rule.

Performance Ratings—Tupalou gets 11 points; Delso, 9 points; Royal Care, 13 points; Decathagal, no points; Bamboo, no points; and S.D. Delight, 11 points.

Price-Factor—Delso is below 5-1 on both the morning line and closing odds; Royal Care and S.D. Delight are below 5-1 on the morning line; Shergaul (already eliminated) has closing odds less than 5-1.

This leaves Tupalou as the only qualified play with a Performance Rating and she paid a whopping $138.00. This race is a perfect example of why we include morning line as well as closing odds in eliminating horses quoted below 5-1. There were four horses in this race with almost identical Performance Ratings and all but one were eliminated by their morning line odds.

The great disparity between the morning line and closing odds of Tupalou was caused by the fact that her stablemate, Fairy Boots (a *PRL* selection with a 26-point rating) was scratched. To obviate the chance of losing a blockbuster payoff in this situation, you might wish to ignore the morning line odds and use the closing odds of the remaining entry horse only.

Example 9
September 28, 1972—Lincoln Downs 1

There are 12 horses in this $1,500 claimer for 3-year-olds and up.

Horse	Dates of Top Three Places	Running Positions				Morning Line Odds	Post Time Odds $1
Oh Never	20 Sept 72	6	7	9	9	15-1	31.20
	28 Aug 72	4	6	3	3		
	5 Aug 72	2	8	8	8		
Hello Spadnik	15 Sept. 72	5	7	7	4	15-1	46.20
	8 Sept 72	11	11	9	8		
	28 Aug 72	1	2	6	7		

Horse	Dates of Top Three Races		Running Positions				Morning Lines Odds	Post Time Odds $1
Tight Belt	20 Sept 72	1	1	2	4		6-1	4.70
	13 Sept 72	2	2	3	4			
	4 Sept 72	5	6	5	5			
Perignon					3		12-1	13.60
Penal Colony	30 Aug. 72	9	9	9	9		20-1	13.30
	18 Aug 72	5	6	8	6			
	1 Aug 72	7	7	8	8			
Mazda					1		8-5	1.40
Chinook Winds					3		8-1	5.80
Fire'n the Boiler	23 Aug 72	6	6	6	6		12-1	10.00
	14 Aug 72	2	5	5	5			
	27 Jul 72	6	6	7	7			
Pawn	14 Sept 72	4	5	4	4		15-1	92.80
	11 Sept 72	2	3	3	4			
	5 Sept 72	3	1	1	1			
Teddy Pick	9 Sept 72	9	8	7	6		15-1	11.00
	30 Aug 72	12	11	11	9			
	6 Apr 71	-	-	-	4			
Green Court	25 Sept 72	2	4	8	8		20-1	48.40
	1 Sept 72	2	3	6	9			
	17 Aug 71	6	9	10	9			
Carried Interest	4 Jan 71	4	6	6	8		4-1	9.90
	19 Dec 70	7	7	8	9			
	8 Dec 70	2	2	1	1			

Preliminary Eliminations—Perignon, Mazda and Chinook Winds finished in the money in their top race. Fire'n the Boiler, Teddy Pick, Green Court, and Carried Interest fail to meet the minimum date rule.

Performance Ratings—Oh Never gets 4 points; Hello Spadnik, 5 points; Tight Belt, 13 points; Penal Colony, no points; Pawn, 14 points.

Price Factor—Tight Belt has closing odds of less than 5-1; Mazda (already eliminated) is below 5-1 on both the morning line and closing odds; Carried Interest (already eliminated) is below 5-1 on the morning line.

Pawn, the top-rated *PRL* choice, is another standout selection as the only other comparably rated horse (Tight Belt) is eliminated by the Date Factor. Pawn paid $187.60 to win and comprised the first half of the highest daily double in North American history—$15,005. The second half was won by Selected Set $46.00 who ran in the money last time out.

Example 10
November 8, 1972—Suffolk Downs 2

There are nine horses in this $1,500 claimer for 3-year-olds and up.

Horse	Dates of Top Three Races		Running Positions			Morning Line Odds	Post Time Odds $1
Subboy	22 Jul 72	4	7	8	8	3-1	2.90
	28 Jun 72	2	2	2	2		
	16 Jun 72	2	2	1	1		
Straight Shooter	27 Oct 72	5	6	7	7	30-1	14.70
	18 Oct 72	2	3	4	4		
	2 Oct 72	2	4	4	5		
Domman	27 Oct 72	2	3	5	7	12-1	29.20
	4 Sept 72	3	2	2	4		
	28 Aug 72	6	4	2	4		
Spinover	26 Oct 72	1	2	4	9	30-1	45.10
	4 Oct 72			4	4		
	30 Sept 72			4	4		
Archon	7 Oct 72	1	1	3	5	30-1	9.80
	30 Sept 72	1	1	5	9		
	25 Sept 72	1	9	9	9		
Wilderness Road	30 Oct 72	5	5	8	9	30-1	27.00
	20 Oct 72	6	6	5	5		
	20 Sept 72	6	9	10	11		
Polmont	(Second by disqualification)				3	7-1	1.40
Its Nowornever	1 Nov 72	1	1	2	4	8-1	1.90
	23 Oct 72	1	2	3	5		
	18 Oct 72	3	2	2	3		
Atrium					3	3-1	3.90

Preliminary Eliminations—Polmont and Atrium finished in the money in their top race. Subboy, Domman, and Archon fail to meet the minimum date rule.

Performance Ratings—Straight Shooter gets 5 points; Spinover, 5 points; Wilderness Road, no points; Its Nowornever, 20 points.

Price Factor—Subboy and Atrium (already eliminated) are below 5-1 on both the morning line and closing odds. Polmont (already eliminated) and Its Nowornever are below 5-1 on closing odds.

This leaves Straight Shooter and Spinover tied with a top Performance Rating of 5 points. Spinover won and returned $92.20. In this situation, both horses could have been played, or just Spinover, the horse with the highest closing tote odds.

Note that Spinover had two calls missing in his middle and bottom races. This is because he ran these races at Pocono Downs in shorter 3½ furlong races. We have not stipulated that a horse must have three complete running lines, believing that this should be left to the discretion of the player.

* * *

This concludes the Basic Plan of *Pro Rated Longshots*. The Intermediate Plan, which follows, shows you how to obtain additional winners by playing horses with more recent races than those required by the minimum date rules.

While this modifies the basic procedure outlined in the Basic Plan, it should make you aware of the options available to you when using progressively tighter date rules. It should also help to explain the codes which identify all of the 1,218 *PRL* winners listed in Appendix 1.

PART 2

The Intermediate Plan

In the Basic Plan, we stuck to a completely mechanical procedure for picking Pro Rated Longshots. Only one date rule was considered in qualifying a horse for play. Why, then, should we complicate things by introducing optional date rules in the Intermediate Plan?

The answer is that optional date rules provide greater flexibility in making selections than is possible when using only one date rule. By adopting stricter Date Factors (which require qualifying horses to have raced more recently), we can play additional winners which would have been missed when sticking to the date rule of the Basic Plan.

In fact, 281 or 23 percent of the 1,218 winning Pro Rated Longshots in Appendix 1 were secured in just this way.

However, most of these 281 winners were obtained by betting horses with lower Performance Ratings against the top-rated *PRL* selection in the race (i.e., the horse with the highest Performance Rating). Various ways to resolve this conflict between the Performance Factor and the Date Factor will be discussed in the section on Supplemental (Non-Top-Rated) Horses.

Other topics covered in the Intermediate Plan include:

Alternative Date Factors—
The effect of substituting a more restrictive date rule for

49

the minimum date rule outlined in the Basic Plan while continuing to play only one horse in a race.

Confirmed Top-Rated Horses—

How extra-powerful betting spots are created by playing top-rated *PRL* selections (those earning the highest Performance Rating) which qualify on two or more date rules.

ALTERNATIVE DATE FACTORS

Now let's examine the other date rules and see how they compare with the date rule, or so-called Minimum Date Factor, outlined in the Basic Plan.

Moderate and Restrictive Date Factors

In Examples 1-10, which illustrate the Basic Plan, we have chosen the horse with the highest Performance Rating (after making Preliminary and Price-Factor Eliminations) as our final selection.

These top-rated horses, as you know, qualified for play on the following minimum date rule:

> Top race within 30 days, middle race within 60 days, bottom race within 90 days; no more than 60 days between successive races.

A loose, non-restrictive Date Factor such as this is very effective in securing higher-priced payoffs and it also pointed out most of the winning *PRL* plays which appear in Appendix 1.

However, a horse which has raced this infrequently could lack sufficient sharpness to win today's race. We said earlier in this section that non-top-rated horses with lower Performance Ratings but more recent races than the top-rated horse, sometimes beat this horse when it only qualified on the minimum date rule.

It was found that most of these supplemental (non-top-rated) winners showed one of the following date, or days-out, patterns:

A moderately restrictive date requirement—

Top race within 20 days, middle race within 50 days, bottom race within 80 days; no more than 30 days between successive races.

A very restrictive date requirement—

Top race within 20 days, three races within 30 days.

Horses qualifying on these different date rules will be identified in the following discussion, and Appendix 1, as:

Minimum Date Factor (Basic Plan)—Step 1.
Moderate Date Factor (Intermediate Plan)—Step 2.
Restrictive Date Factor (Intermediate Plan)—Step 3.

Just as the Step 1 horse is never played unless it has the highest Performance Rating of any horse meeting the minimum date requirements, so, too, the Step 2 and Step 3 horses are not played unless they have the highest Performance Rating of any horse meeting the Moderate or Restrictive Date Rules, respectively.

Choosing the Best Date Factor

Before discussing Confirmed Top-Rated and Supplemental (non-top-rated) horses, let's examine the effect of substituting a more restrictive date rule for the minimum requirement while continuing to play only one horse in each race (the top-rated horse qualifying on whichever date rule we selected).

Here are the totals for 1972 with the three different Date Factors:

Number of *PRL* Winners When Using:

Minimum Date Factor (Step 1)	937
Moderate Date Factor (Step 2)	823
Restrictive Date Factor (Step 3)	510

The reason that these figures so far exceed the winning total for the workout year of 1,218 is that many horses qualified on two or more Date Factors. This will be explained shortly.

As we switch to successively tighter date rules, we cut down both on the number of plays and the number of winners. We might also expect the average payoff to be lower, but this is not the case as the following figures show:

Average payoff on Step 1 winners–$25.80
Average payoff on Step 2 winners–$26.40
Average payoff on Step 3 winners–$26.20

As you can see from these figures, it makes little difference which date rule we select insofar as the average payoff is concerned. However, the winning percentage should be increased as we switch to progressively tighter date rules.

If this is so, why should one play anything except Step 3 horses, or at the very most, Step 2 and 3 horses?

Because many players, especially longshot players, do not want to restrict their betting activity to this extent. Since the Minimum (Step 1) Date Factor picks more winners than the alternative date rules, switching to those rules necessarily causes one to miss out on the high-priced *PRL* winners which only qualify on the Minimum (Step 1) Date Requirement.

A prime example is Sy's Theme who paid $119.60 while winning the second half of Gulfstream Park's record-breaking daily double (Example 6). Sy's Theme had not raced for exactly 30 days and hence qualified only on the minimum date rules.[14]

The Step 1, or minimum, date rule is also especially effective in the "off months" when horses are switching from northern tracks to southern winter tracks in the fall and moving northward again in the spring. Traveling time and training interruptions can create considerable gaps between races; many of these rested horses pay tremendous prices when they win at new meetings.

The counter argument runs like this: It is always easier to beat a race than to beat the races, and the fewer plays the better the chances of earning a profit.

More specifically, horses with more-recent races should outperform those with less-recent ones and we should therefore be able to increase our profit percentage by switching to progressively tighter date rules.

Quite possibly this is true. But when playing a longshot system the psychological impact of missing blockbuster payoffs such as Sy's Theme can be devastating. That's why we advise you to think twice before switching exclusively to Step 2 or Step 3 horses. By leaving all options available, you can enjoy maximum flexibility and obtain many winners which you would miss when sticking to just one date rule.

CONFIRMED TOP-RATED HORSES

We will now explain why top-rated horses qualifying on two or more date factors are extra powerful plays.

Top-rated horses qualifying on both the minimum and moderate date rules are known as Double-Top-Rated horses or Step 1 2 plays.

Top-rated horses qualifying on the minimum, moderate, and restrictive date rules are known as Triple-Top-Rated Horses or Step 1 2 3 plays.

Double-Top-Rated Horses

Choosing between Step 1 and Step 2 horses is not as difficult as it seems. This is because most top-rated horses qualifying on the Minimum (Step 1) Date Factor also satisfy the

Moderate (Step 2) Date Factor. These are known as Double-Top-Rated or Step 1 2 plays.

During the workout year 1972, 937 or 77 percent of the 1,218 *PRL* winners were top-rated Step 1 plays; *714 or 76 percent of these Step 1 winners were double-top-rated horses* which qualified on the moderate (Step 2) date rule in addition to the minimum date requirement.

When a top-rated *PRL* selection satisfies the moderately restrictive date requirement there is no conflict between Step 1 and Step 2 horses because:

> Any *top-rated* horse which qualifies as a Step 2 play automatically qualifies as a Step 1 play, too.

And since—all things being equal (class, consistency, odds, previous competition)—a horse with more-recent races should beat one with less-recent races, it also follows that:

> A top-rated horse which qualifies as both Step 1 and Step 2 is a stronger play than a top-rated horse which qualifies as a Step 1 selection only.

These double-top-rated horses are identified in the List of Winners (Appendix 1) with the designation, "1 2."

Returning to Example Races 1-10, all of the winners except Sy's Theme (Example 6) and Coraggioso (Example 7) were double-top-rated (Step 1 2) horses. [15]

By restricting your play to Step 1 2 horses (top-rated PRL selections which qualify on both the moderate and minimum date rules) you not only should reduce the number of plays (by about 30 percent) but also should increase your percentage of profit.

Triple-Top-Rated Horses

We have said that 714 or 76 percent of the 937 top-rated

(Step 1) winners were double-top-rated (Step 1 2) plays. The number of horses which further qualified for the Very Restrictive (Step 3) Date Factor was considerably less, as might be expected; it amounted to 292—only 30% of the 937 top-rated winners.

However, when a top-rated horse does meet the stringent Step 3 requirements it becomes the most powerful of all possible plays. That is why we referred to Bee Bee Bee (Example 4) as a standout PRL selection—he was a triple-top-rated (Step 1 2 3) winner who met the very restrictive (Step 3) date rules. Pawn, in Example 9, was another triple-top-rated winner.

The conclusions reached for Step 2 horses, when comparing them to Step 1 horses, also apply to the Step 3 horse compared to Steps 1 and 2, since:

> A top-rated horse which qualifies as Step 3 automatically qualifies as Step 1 and 2 also.

And by the same reasoning:

> A top-rated horse qualifying on the restrictive date rule (Step 3) is a stronger play than one which qualifies as Step 1 and 2 or Step 1 only.

The triple-top-rated or Step 1 2 3 horse is a perfect medium for a spot-play[16] approach. Limiting your play to these selections should reduce your amount of action by more than 50 percent but it promises very interesting profit possibilities.

SUPPLEMENTAL (NON-TOP-RATED) HORSES

As long as we stick to one date rule there is no problem about which horse to play. We simply choose the horse with the highest Performance Rating which qualifies on the Step 1 (or Step 2, or Step 3) date rules. Our problem is also simplified by the abundance of double- and triple-top-rated horses.

But when we start to juggle two or three different date requirements we face the possibility of choosing between horses or perhaps playing more than one horse in a race.

The problem arises when a horse with more recent races has a lower Performance Rating than one with less recent races.[17] To be sure you understand this distinction, take the following example:

Horse	Performance Rating	Days Since Top Three Races
A	14	30–60–90
B	11	20–50–80
C	8	10–20–30

Horse A, which is top-rated, only meets the minimum date requirement (Step 1); Horse B, with the second highest rating, meets the moderate date rule (Step 2); and Horse C, with the third highest rating, meets the very restrictive date rule (Step 3). Horse B is therefore the highest-rated Step 2 selection and Horse C is the highest-rated Step 3 play.[18]

Had Horse B or C won the race they would have been Supplemental (Non-Top-Rated) Winners because Horse A was the top-rated selection.

During the workout year 1972, 281 or 23 percent of the 1,218 Pro-Rated Longshot winners were supplemental (non-top-rated) plays; i.e., they were the highest rated Step 2, Step 3, or Step 2 3 horses which qualified in the same race as a top-rated (Step 1) selection.[19]

Before deciding how to resolve such conflicts we can assure you that the problem is not as thorny as it might seem. The fundamental differences between the Step 2 and Step 3 selections suggest quite different solutions.

Conflicts Between Step 1 and 2 Horses[20]

Referring to our table on the preceding page, let's look at some possible ways to handle the situation where a top-rated Step 1 selection meets a lower-rated Step 2 horse with more-recent races. In our example, Horse A (Step1) has 14 points and Horse B (Step 2) has 11 points.

Here are some of the alternatives:

1. Choose one Date Factor (Step 1 or Step 2) and stick to it in all races.
2. Pass the race.
3. Resolve the conflict by your own preference or other handicapping factors (class, speed, etc.).
4. Play the horse with the highest morning line and/or closing tote odds.
5. Play both horses (especially when 10-1 or more).

The choice in the final analysis depends on the individual player. Alternative #1 is certainly the simplest. However, flexibility is often preferable to simplicity when seeking high-priced payoffs.

That's why we prefer Alternatives #4 or #5 in most races. Common sense should tell us to choose a Step 2 horse with 14 points at 25-1 over a Step 1 horse with 15 points at only 5-1, But if they were both 10-1, 15-1, or 20-1, it could be equally foolish not to play them both.

Sticking to one Date Factor exclusively will keep you out of the switches—no doubt about it—but the high prices paid by *Pro Rated Longshots* at least suggest the alternative of occasionally. switching Date Factors or even playing two horses in the same race.

Example 11, which follows, illustrates a supplemental Step 2 play which was not the top-rated selection in its field.

Example 11
December 20, 1972—Laurel 1

There are 12 horses in this $5,000 claimer for 2-year-olds.

Horse	Dates of Three Top Races		Running Positions				Morning Line Odds	Post Time Odds $1
Irish Cloud	6 Nov 72	11	11	11	11		30-1	88.90
	16 Aug 72	5	8	8	8			
Kim Michelle					3		6-1	3.30
Repose	2 Nov 72	6	7	7	6		8-1	12.70
	25 Oct 72	9	8	7	6			
	11 Oct 72	10	8	6	5			
Red Hank	24 Nov 72	5	7	10	10		15-1	48.30
	3 Nov 72	3	11	12	12			
	25 Oct 72	6	3	3	5			
All There Is	22 Nov 72	7	9	9	9		15-1	105.90
	7 Nov 72	4	3	2	2			
	25 Jul 72	11	10	9	7			
Cavan Coup	14 Dec 72	7	8	6	5		12-1	10.10
	6 Dec 72	11	9	10	10			
	3 Nov 72	8	10	10	8			
Lahar					3		8-1	11.00
Bahamas Solo	24 Nov 72	6	8	9	9		15-1	34.20
	10 Nov 72	9	12	12	12			
	3 Nov 72	7	5	4	4			
Trumbull	6 Dec 72	7	6	5	4		8-5	1.20
	27 Nov 72	4	3	2	1			
	10 Nov 72	7	4	2	2			
Lark Wood	4 Dec 72				1		8-1	12.10
Barnesville Belle	7 Dec 72	9	8	7	7		20-1	71.60
	27 Nov 72	4	3	5	7			
	15 Nov 72		9	7	3			
Alice's Idol					2		4-1	8.60

Preliminary Eliminations—Kim Michelle, Lahar, Lark Wood, and Alice's Idol finished in the money in their top race. Irish Cloud has fewer than three races. Repose and All There Is do not meet the minimum date rule.

Performance Ratings—Red Hank (Step 1) gets 3 points; Cavan Coup (Step 1), no points; Bahamas Solo (Step 1), no points; Trumbull (Step 2), 10 points; Barnesville Belle (Step 2), 2 points.

Price Factor—Kim Michelle (already eliminated) has closing odds below 5-1; Alice's Idol (already eliminated) is below 5-1 on the morning line; Trumbull is below 5-1 both on morning line and closing tote odds.

Only two horses are left with Performance Ratings—Red Hank, the top-rated horse (Step 1) and Barnesville Belle, the highest rated Step 2 play. Barnesville Belle returned a $145.20 win payoff.

Note that Red Hank had not raced for 26 days while Barnesville Belle had raced only 13 days ago—a compelling argument for playing both horses (Step 1 and 2) at these odds.

Conflicts With Step 3 Horses

We now consider how to resolve conflicts with Step 3 horses—those which have raced once within 20 days and three times in the past 30 days.

We noted in the preceding section that while 76 percent of the top-rated winners qualifying on the Minimum Date Factor (Step 1) also met the moderate date requirement (Step 2), only 30 percent of these winners further qualified for the very restrictive (Step 3) date rule. This obviously poses a new sort of problem.

Let's refer again to our example where Horse A (Step 1) has 14 points; Horse B (Step 2), 11 points; and Horse C (Step 3), 8 points.

Where a top-rated Step 1 play (such as Horse A) meets a supplemental (non-top-rated) Step 3 play (Horse C), the conflict could be resolved in one of the ways suggested for Step 1 and Step 2 conflicts. However, the minimum and moderate date rules are essentially similar, whereas the very restrictive date rule is practically in a class by itself. We therefore suggest a different solution.

Most horses have not raced three times within 30 days. Those who have are spot plays and should be considered accordingly.

We recommend that when a top-rated Step 1, or Step 1 2, horse appears in the same race as the supplemental (non-top-rated) Step 3 selection (i.e., the Step 3 horse with the highest Performance Rating), the latter horse should be played separately—in addition to, but not in place of, the former, basic selection.

For example you could place your regular bet (say $10) on the former horse and put a saver (say $2) on the latter.

Example 12, below, illustrates a race won by a non-top-rated Step 3 horse.

Example 12
August 11, 1972—Saratoga 8

There are ten horses in the Bernard Baruch Handicap ($20,000 added) for 3-year-olds and up.

Horses	Dates of Top Three Races	Running Positions				Morning Line Odds	Post Time Odds $1
Chrisaway	5 Aug 72	4	7	7	6	20-1	52.30
	23 Jul 72	5	4	5	3		
	13 Jul 72	2	3	5	5		
Galeon II					1	15-1	52.00
Acclimatization					1	8-1	10.20
Apollo Nine					2	10-1	4.40
Larceny Kid	29 Jul 72	2	3	3	6	8-1	9.40
	11 Jul 72	4	3	4	2		
	4 Jul 72	4	3	2	1		
Shelter Bay					1	10-1	6.80
Urgent Message	29 Jul 72	10	9	7	7	12-1	10.40
	19 Jul 72	6	6	6	4		
	8 Jul 72	8	11	10	11		
Malwak	1 Aug 72	8	7	6	4	8-1	8.10
	23 Jul 72	11	5	1	1		
	17 Jun 72	5	5	5	5		

Horses	Dates of Top Three Races	Running Positions	Morning Line Odds	Post Time Odds $1
North Flight		1	4-1	4.80
Dubassoff		1	5-2	2.20

Preliminary Eliminations—Galeon II, Acclimatization, Apollo Nine, Shelter Bay, North Flight, and Dubassoff finished in the money in their top race.

Performance Ratings—Chrisaway gets 4 points; Larceny Kid, 13 points; Urgent Message, no points; and Malwak, 6 points.

Price Factor—North Flight and Dubassoff (already eliminated) are below 5-1 on both morning line and closing toteboard odds. Apollo Nine (already eliminated) is below 5-1 on closing odds.

Larceny Kid (a Step 2 play) is top-rated with 13 points; Malwak (a Step 1 play) has 6 points; however, Chrisaway as the only qualified play on the Restrictive Date Rule, is the top-rated Step 3 play with 4 points. His win payoff was $106.60.

Note that Chrisaway had three races in 29 days while Larceny Kid's bottom race was run 38 days ago.

At these odds you could certainly have put a saver on Chrisaway, a very nice Step 3 winner.

Special Step 3 Spot Plays

In revealing the winning mystique of *Pro Rated Longshots* we have shown that the most important factor or motivating force is the Performance Rating. It is the quantity and quality of running positions which give our horse the capability to win. The Date Factor, especially with Step 1 and Step 2 plays, is little more than an elimination rule rather than a positive asset.

When we enter the realm of Step 3 plays, however, the very fact that a horse has raced so recently serves as a new and different plus-factor. Horses with three very recent races, especially when their top race did not take too much out of them, are very powerful plays considering their worthwhile odds.

For this reason we have included within the Step 3 category a special type of horse which has no Performance points at all. Unlike the top-rated Step 3 horse which also qualifies as a Step 1 and Step 2 play, this special horse can only qualify as a Step 3 selection, since it lacks the one-point minimum Performance Rating required for Step 1 and Step 2 horses.

Here are the rules for this special Step 3 spot play:

1. A Step 3 horse can qualify for play with no Performance points provided there are no other Step 3 horses (after Preliminary and Price-Factor eliminations) with 1 or more points in the same race.
2. Where two or more Step 3 horses, with no points, qualify in the same race, choose the horse whose bottom race was run most recently.

Note that Rule 2 substitutes the date of the bottom race for the number of Performance points in separating these special Step 3 horses.

Winners in Appendix 1 qualifying on this special Step 3 spot play are identified with an asterisk after the number (3*).

Example 13 shows how a winner was picked by this Step 3 spot play.

Example 13
June 9, 1972—Liberty Bell 5

There are eight horses in this $5,000 claimer for 4-year-olds and up.

Horse	Dates of Top Three Races	Running Positions	Morning Line Odds	Post Time Odds $1
Nova Caesarea		2	2-1	.90

Horses	Dates of Top Three Races	Running Positions				Morning Line Odds	Post Time Odds $1
Duke San	29 May 72	6	6	7	5	15-1	9.90
	28 Apr 72	6	7	7	6		
	22 Apr 72	8	8	8	8		
Clay	27 May 72	7	5	4	4	12-1	14.90
	23 May 72	7	5	5	5		
	11 May 72	8	8	6	5		
Where Ruler					2	4-1	6.80
I'm Irving	27 May 72	7	7	5	4	3-1	6.10
	20 May 72	3	3	5	4		
	13 May 72	9	7	4	2		
Gypsy Rattler	5 Jun 72	7	7	6	5	12-1	10.60
	25 May 72	4	4	5	7		
	15 May 72	4	6	7	7		
Carousel Clown	23 May 72	4	5	6	4	5-1	6.10
	24 Apr 72	9	8	6	5		
	13 Apr 72	6	6	6	6		
Cap Sail	18 May 72	9	10	10	8	6-1	25.10
	10 May 72	1	1	1	1		
	3 May 72	2	2	2	2		

Preliminary Eliminations—Nova Caesarea and Where Ruler finished in the money in their top race.

Performance Ratings—Duke San (Step 1) gets no points; Clay (Step 3), no points; I'm Irving (Step 3), 4 points; Gypsy Rattler (Step 3), no points; Carousel Clown (Step 2), no points; and Cap Sail (Step 1), 20 points.

Price Factor—I'm Irving is below 3-1 on the morning line.

Cap Sail is top rated with 20 points. After the elimination of I'm Irving on the Price Factor, Clay and Gypsy Rattler (with no points) are the only remaining Step 3 plays. Since the latter horse has a more recent bottom race than the former horse (May 15 to May 11) and since there are no other Step 3 horses with one or more points, Gypsy Rattler qualifies for the Step 3 Spot Play. He returned $23.20 to win.

* * *

PART 3

The Advanced Plan

ALTERNATIVE PERFORMANCE RATINGS

When applying Performance Ratings to *PRL* selections, the same numerical value has been assigned to all 11 calls for horses running first, second, or third. We shall refer to it, in this section, as the Equal Call Performance Rating.

While the Equal Call Performance Rating is the most effective and most flexible rating, it is not perfect. For example:

1. It fails to recognize that some calls are more important than others in determining the horse's chances of winning today.
2. The 3-2-1 scoring system for horses running first, second, or third puts too much emphasis on leading—especially at the earlier or intermediate calls.
3. It exaggerates the value of a wire-to-wire front-running win in either the middle or bottom race. Such an effort earns 12 points—more than most horses score for running second or third at five or more calls in two or all three races.

The alternative Performance Ratings which follow are designed expressly to overcome these objections.

65

The Outer Call Performance Rating

The Outer Call Performance Rating recognizes that the three intermediate calls of the horse's top race, and the finishing positions of its middle and bottom races, are more important than the other six calls (Objection 1, above).

In the drawing which follows, the outside calls of the horse's three-race chart have been separated from the inside ones. It is these outer calls, as explained above, which are considered to be the most important in judging the horse's winning chances today.

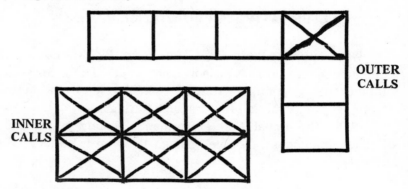

The Outer Call Performance Rating also assigns points for running first, second, or third at any call. But since the points are allotted to only five calls instead of 11, a 5-3-2 scoring plan has been substituted for the 3-2-1 scoring of the Equal Call Rating.

Considering only the five outer calls, give the horse:

5 points each time it was running (or finished)first.
3 points each time it was running (or finished) second.
2 points each time it was running (or finished) third.

The total point score can range from a high of 25 points to a low of 2 points. As in the Equal Call Rating, however, there is an exception for dead-heats. These are scored as follows:

Tie for first in middle or bottom race—4 points.
Tie for second in middle or bottom race—2½ points.
Tie for third in middle or bottom race—1 point.

Considering ties, therefore, the lowest possible score with the Outer Call Rating is 1 point.

Since the outer calls are more closely related to the horse's winning chances than the inner ones, the Outer Call Rating has a higher winning percentage than the Equal Call Rating, especially in the lower payoff range ($12 to $20). But it misses many high-priced winners whose hidden form is revealed only by the inside calls.

As a perfect case in point, consider Sy's Theme (Example 6). Since all of her 6 points came from the inner calls she could not have qualified for play on the Outer Call Rating.

Following is a comparison of mutually exclusive winners picked by the Outer Call and Equal Call Performance Ratings. It covers the period from January 1 to March 31, 1972, and is limited to payoffs of $20 or more. The left-hand figure shows the number of wins, the right-hand figure the combined total of winning payoffs.

	Outer Call Rating	Equal Call Rating
Top-Rated Winners (Types 1, 1-2, 1-2-3)	37–$1,350.40	26–$1,137.00
Non-Top-Rated Winners (Types 2, 3, 2-3)	5– 141.60	7– 433.40
Total Winners:	42–$1,492.00	33–$1,570.40

Note that while the Outer Call Rating picked more winners, the average payoff of the Equal Call Rating was much higher. In addition to Sy's Theme $119.60, there were three other $100-plus winners and five payoffs between $50 and $100 missed by the Outer Call Rating. Also note the tremendous difference in average payoffs for the Supplemental (Non-Top-Rated) Winners.

However, if $12 to $20 payoffs had been included in this comparison, the margin of total winners picked by the Outer Call over the Equal Call Rating would probably have been greater.[21]

The chief drawback of the Outer Call Rating is that it puts too much emphasis on the top race as compared to the middle and bottom races. In fact, more points are allotted to the top race than to the other two races combined.

Another disadvantage of the Outer Call Rating, not shown by this comparison, is that of Performance-Rating Ties. There are many more ties in point scores for both top and supplemental ratings with the Outer Call than with the Equal Call Rating because it uses only five calls instead of 11 to rate the PRL selections.

No fewer than 17 of 42 winners picked exclusively by the Outer Call Rating (see comparison, above) were involved in such ties, while the corresponding figure was only five for the Equal Call Rating. Ties are especially common when a horse receives points for only one of the five outer calls.

While the Outer Call Rating is not intended as a substitute for the Equal Call Rating you should be aware of its advantages, especially if you want a higher winning percentage. Example 14 shows how a winner was picked by only the Outer Call Rating.

Example 14
February 23, 1972—Bowie 2

There are 12 horses in this $3,000 claimer for 3-year-olds and up.

Horse	Dates of Top Three Races	Running Positions				Morning Line Odds	Post Time Odds $1
Pat the Nurse	11 Feb 72	10	10	10	10	30-1	24.50
	7 Feb 72	7	8	9	9		
	15 Nov 71	10	10	10	10		
Wats New Vimy					2	4-1	2.90

Horses	Dates of Top Three Races	Running Positions				Morning Line Odds	Post Time Odds $1
Empire Lou	11 Feb 72	9	9	10	10	15-1	32.50
	4 Feb 72	10	11	12	12		
	12 Jan 72	2	1	1	4		
Marden	16 Feb 72	8	8	8	9	20-1	17.20
	20 Jan 72	12	11	9	8		
	7 Jan 72	9	9	8	8		
Thank You Sir					1	8-1	8.00
Piano Annie					3	8-1	9.00
Longwood's Dare	9 Feb 72	10	10	8	8	8-1	33.00
	25 Jan 72	12	10	6	5		
	20 Dec 71	11	10	9	9		
Hyphen Rulla					1	5-2	5.50
Tul Echo	9 Feb 72	8	7	6	6	6-1	17.10
	26 Jan 72	9	8	4	4		
	12 Jan 72	8	4	2	1		
Hey Maggie	16 Feb 72	9	7	6	7	20-1	41.80
	3 Feb 72	7	4	5	4		
	22 Jan 72	11	10	9	8		
One of Many	31 Jan 72	2	2	6	6	2-1	7.60
	19 Jan 72	1	1	1	1		
	6 Jan 72	7	1	2	3		
Gentle Spring	16 Feb 72	12	12	9	4	15-1	3.70
	24 Jan 72	12	10	8	8		
	18 Jan 72	11	10	10	9		

Preliminary Eliminations—Wats New Vimy, Thank You Sir, Piano Annie, and Hyphen Rulla finished in the money in their top race. Pat the Nurse fails to meet the minimum date rules.

Performance Ratings—Empire Lou gets 8 points; Tul Echo, 5 points; One of Many, 22 points; all other horses, no points.

Price Factor—One of Many is below 5-1 on the morning line.

Empire Lou, with 8 points, is the final selection on the Equal Call Rating—he ran tenth. However, on the Outer Call Rating, Tul Echo gets 5 points and Empire Lou no points. Tul

Echo, as the only rated horse (quoted at 5-1 or higher) on the Outer Call approach paid $36.20 to win.

Since Empire Lou got all of his Equal Call rating points on the inner calls he scored no points on the Outer Call Rating Plan.

* * *

The list of winners picked exclusively by this alternative Rating Plan (January 1–March 31, 1972) appears in Appendix 2.

The Weighted Call Performance Rating

The Weighted Call Performance Rating minimizes the distortions outlined in Objections 2 and 3. It is a compromise between the Equal Call and Outer Call Ratings in that it includes all 11 calls but gives much greater weight to the outer ones.

Its chief feature, though, is that it gives horses the same rating for running first, second, or third at any given call.

The Weighted Call Rating separates the familiar three-race running-line diagram into three parts: (1) Finishing positions of the middle and bottom races; (2) Three intermediate calls of the top race; (3) Inside calls.

3	3	3	✕
2	2	2	5
2	2	2	5

As you can see from the above drawing, a horse receives:

5 points each time it finished in the money in its middle or bottom race.

3 points each time it was running one, two, or three at the intermediate calls of its top race.

2 points each time it was running one, two, or three at one of the inside calls.

The point score with the Weighted Call Performance Rating can range from a high of 31 to a low of 2 points, and the minimum score is not affected by dead-heats for first, second, or third in the middle or bottom races.

Such ties are scored as follows:

Tie for first or second in middle or bottom race—5 points.
Tie for third in middle or bottom race—2½ points.

Since it makes no difference whether the horse finishes first, second or third in these races, the score is lowered only when it ties for the latter position.

The winning percentage and average payoffs with the Weighted Call Rating fall somewhere between those obtained with the Equal Call and Outer Call Rating Plans. In other words:

Equal Call has: Lower win percent, higher payoffs.
Outer Call has: Higher win percent, lower payoffs.
Weighted Call has: Medium win percent, medium payoffs.

Sy's Theme $119.60 (Example 6) is again a good case in point. She was top rated by a wide margin with the Equal Call, received no rating with the Outer Call, and was top-rated by a very narrow margin with the Weighted Call.

Example 15 shows how a high-priced winner was picked by the Weighted Call Rating but missed by the other two rating plans.

Example 15
October 10, 1972—Laurel 5

There are nine horses in this $9,500 claimer for 2-year-olds.

Horse	Dates of Top Three Races	Running Positions				Morning Line Odds	Post Time Odds $1
Juss Fishing	29 Sep 72	5	6	5	5	10-1	13.60
	21 Sep 72	6	3	2	1		
	13 Sep 72	4	3	4	4		
Tutu	2 Oct 72	4	5	7	7	4-1	3.30
	13 Sep 72	10	9	5	3		
	4 Sep 72	6	6	5	4		
Little Marty	2 Oct 72	6	4	4	5	10-1	10.60
	25 Sep 72	6	6	6	4		
	16 Aug 72	1	1	7	7		
Pomme					3	3-1	3.30
Shoot N' Dash					1	5-1	7.30
Ballet Master					1	4-1	5.30
Mooreroom	2 Oct 72	7	7	8	9	20-1	30.70
	2 Sep 72	5	5	3	3		
	22 Aug 72	4	4	4	3		
Smashing	2 Oct 72	8	6	5	6	20-1	49.00
	14 Sep 72	3	1	2	1		
	1 Sep 72	7	5	4	4		
Cut Up Kitsy					2	6-1	3.30

Preliminary Eliminations—Pomme, Shoot N' Dash, Ballet Master, Cut Up Kitsy finished in the money in their top race.

Performance Ratings—Juss Fishing gets 7 points; Tutu, 1 point; Little Marty, 6 points; Mooreroom, 3 points; Smashing, 9 points.

Price Factor—Tutu is below 5-1 on morning line and closing toteboard odds.

On the Equal Call Rating Plan, Smashing is top-rated with 9 points.

On the Outer Call Rating Plan, Juss Fishing and Smashing tie for the top rating with 5 points (but since Juss Fishing has three races in 30 days he has the highest Step 3 rating).

On the Weighted Call Rating Plan, Juss Fishing gets 11

points; Tutu, 5 points; Little Marty, 4 points; Mooreroom, 12 points; Smashing, 11 points.

Mooreroom, the top-rated selection on the Weighted Call Rating Plan, returned $63.40 to win. Juss Fishing ran sixth and Smashing finished eighth.

This example race highlights the essential difference in emphasis between the Equal Call and Weighted Call Rating Plans. Since Mooreroom was running third at all three in-the-money calls, he got a very low score on the Equal Call Rating Plan. But the fact that he was the only horse to finish in the money in both his middle and bottom races was sufficient to give him the top rating on the Weighted Call Rating Plan. Juss Fishing and Smashing had higher ratings on the Equal Call and Outer Call Rating Plans because they had more in-the-money calls and were running first or second at half or more of these calls.

In addition to showing the different emphasis of the Weighted Call Rating Plan, this example race also proves that no single rating plan always get the high-priced winners.

* * *

The advantages of the Weighted Call Performance Rating are lessened somewhat by the fact that it overemphasizes horses which finished second, or especially third, in their middle or bottom race.

As an everyday, all-purpose rating plan the Equal Call Performance Rating is clearly best. However, you ought to recognize the advantages of the two alternative Performance Ratings, especially when they pick horses which agree with your own handicapping choices, or which are held at very attractive odds.

Other Alternative Performance Ratings

The number and variety of other Performance Ratings are almost infinite. Here are just a few:

1. Equal Call, Equal Running Position, Rating—
   Award one point to the horse each time it was running one, two, or three at any call.
2. Weighted Call, Weighted Running Position, Rating—
   Give the horse 9-6-3 points for finishing one, two, or three in its middle or bottom race; 6-4-2 points for running one, two or three at each of three intermediate calls of top race; 3-2-1 points for running one, two, or three at each of the six inside calls.
3. Weighted In-Stretch Call Rating—
   Scored exactly like the Weighted Call Rating except that the horse receives 5 points instead of 3 for running one, two, or three at the stretch call of its top race, and 3 points instead of 2 for running one, two, or three at the stretch call of its middle or bottom race.

Whichever Performance Rating you decide to play, the most important thing is to turn it to your advantage and, above all, NOT to get caught in the switches.

ALTERNATIVE PRICE FACTORS

When considering alternative Price Factors we must realize that no system of minimum odds is perfect. The 5-1 rule, like all others, is arbitrary and can sometimes lose the very high-priced winner it is designed to protect.

For example, a top-rated horse leaves the gate at 5-1 or 6-1, while a very close second-rated horse is quoted at 20-1, 30-1, or 50-1. When the latter horse wins, one might understandably question the logic not only of the Price Factor but of the entire *Pro Rated Longshots.*

The alternative Price Factors which follow are designed to prevent this sort of situation, but you must realize that to get something you have to give something, too. The choice is yours.

The Top-Two-Rating Price Factor

Here's the plan in a nutshell:

> Determine which two horses have the highest Performance Ratings and play the one going postward at the greatest odds. (For off-track play substitute scratch sheet for toteboard, or use best available morning line).

The list of additional winners picked by this alternative Price Factor appears in Appendix 3. The period checked was from October 1 to December 31, 1972. Payoffs of less than $20 were not considered and the survey was restricted to top-rated (Step 1) horses.

SUMMARY OF ADDITIONAL WINNERS

Month	$20-$30	$30-$50	$50-$100	$100-Plus	Total
Oct.	4	2	1	1	8
Nov.	2	6	6	2	16
Dec.	5	4	2		11
Total:	11	12	9	3	35

During the same three months of our survey year, the 5-1 Minimum Price Factor of the Basic Plan picked 168 winners at $20 or more. The Top-Two-Rating Price Factor therefore increased this total by about 20 percent. Its percentage of additional winners in the higher price brackets ($30 to $50, $50 to $100, etc.) was correspondingly greater.

How shall we judge this alternative Price Factor? On the positive side of the ledger its thrust toward higher-priced winners raises the average payoff level, which furthers the very purpose of *Pro Rated Longshots.*

On the negative side, its month-to-month record is somewhat erratic, and the number of extra winners leaves something to be desired since many winners already picked by the 5-1 Minimum Price Factor would be eliminated by this approach, especially in the $12 to $20 category.

The Top-Two-Rating Price Factor is recommended only if you are willing to pay for your higher-priced winners with a lower winning percentage.

The Performance-Price Factor

What we said about the alternative Price Factor described above is just as true of this approach. You give a lot to get a lot. The Performance-Price Factor incorporates the horse's morning-line or closing toteboard odds into the rating score. For example:

	Performance Rating (1)	Morning-Line Odds (2)	Total (1 x 2)
Horse A	10	5	50
Horse B	3	15	45
Horse C	2	30	60

In this example, Horse C with only 2 points is the final selection because its morning-line odds multiplied by its Performance Rating gives it the highest point score.

This approach gets some very high-priced winners missed by the 5-1 Minimum Price Factor, but it often chooses horses with very low Performance Ratings and it also eliminates many lower- and medium-priced winners, thereby lowering the win percentage.

Toteboard odds can be substituted for morning-line odds if you are at the track. This variation has the double advantage of greater accuracy and still higher payoffs, but it requires constant watching of the toteboard and it magnifies the drawback of the morning-line multiplier (low winning percentage).

The Performance-Price Factor offers great rewards but it requires even greater patience in waiting for winners.

10-1 Minimum Closing Odds Price Factor

This is handled exactly like the conventional 5-1 Minimum Odds Price Factor except that minimum closing tote odds of 10-1 are substituted for the present 5-1 minimum. In other words, the horse must have the following minimum odds to qualify for play:

Morning-line odds   5-1
Toteboard odds   10-1

The morning-line odds minimum is not raised for the simple reason that too many 5-1, 6-1, and 8-1 selections pegged by public selectors and track handicappers wind up paying $20, $30, or more.

This approach certainly solves the problem of the second-rated 30-1 horse beating out the top-rated 5-1 horse, but it has one serious disadvantage—it eliminates every single winner in the $12 to $20 category. In the year of our survey, as you recall, this price bracket accounted for just over half of the 1,218 *PRL* winners.

The Proportional Odds Price Factor

One other Price Factor offers perhaps the best, and probably the most flexible, alternative to the 5-1 Minimum Odds Factor of the Basic Plan. This is the Proportional Odds Price Factor.

Proportional odds are post-time odds related to the field size. In a 10-horse field, for example, our selection must beat nine other horses. Assuming all horses to be of equal ability, its winning chances are 9-1. In a 12-horse race, its chances of winning are 11-1; in a 6-horse race, 5-1.

This table highlights the essential difference between the 5-1 Minimum Odds and the Proportional Odds Price Factors:

MINIMUM ODDS REQUIREMENT

Field Size	5-1 Minimum Odds Price Factor	Proportional Odds Price Factor
6	5-1	5-1
7	5-1	6-1
8	5-1	7-1
9	5-1	8-1
10	5-1	9-1
11	5-1	10-1
12	5-1	11-1

Note: It is suggested that minimum odds of 5-1 be retained for fields of five or less with the proportional Odds Price Factor.

By tailoring the minimum odds to the field size, we can facilitate the job of picking overlays rather than underlays with *PRL*. It is apparent, from this table, that a selection going postward at 5-1 is not an overlay in larger fields.

We have not compared the results of the Proportional Odds Price Factor with other Price Factors but believe that it should add approximately as many high-priced winners as the Top-Two-Rated Price Factor, while retaining more of the lower priced payoffs.

Let's look at a few examples to see how the Proportional Odds Price Factor simplifies the selection process and helps to retain key high-priced winners.

In Example 5, a 12-horse race, the minimum Proportional Odds are 11-1. Margie C., whose Performance Rating (18 points) was a close second to the 20 points earned by Noble Duel, went postward at 9.30 to 1. These odds eliminated her on the Proportional Odds Price Factor. (Had she earned 21 or more points with the 5-1 Minimum Odds Price Factor we would have lost our highest-priced winner of the entire year.)

Another advantage of the Proportional Odds Price Factor is that it minimizes the need for the concurrent price rule requiring a selection to be 5-1 or more on the morning line. Example 8, a 12-horse race, illustrates this point perfectly.

Tupalou, the winner, had 11 points; Royal Care with 13 points and S.D. Delight with 11 points were eliminated by the Price Factor of the Basic Plan because their morning line odds were only 4-1. However, as the latter two horses went postward at 5-1, they only missed qualifying for play by a very narrow margin (just one point on their morning line odds).

This borderline situation could more easily have been resolved by the Proportional Odds Price Factor as both horses went postward at odds way below the 11-1 minimum requirement.

One other point—the determinant of field size when using the Proportional Odds Price Factor is NOT the number of horses in the race but the number of betting units. The number is usually the same, but when two horses are part of an entry, or coupled in the field (as in races with more than 12 horses), there are fewer betting units than horses.

In Example 7, there were nine horses but only eight betting units since Gypsy Blade and Jimminy Gosh were coupled as an entry. Therefore, the minimum odds on the Proportional Odds Price Factor were reduced to 7-1 from 8-1.

HANDICAPPING VS. SYSTEM PLAY

Pro Rated Longshots in its original and alternative forms is completely mechanical. Nothing is left to judgment. This suggests one other alternative—to include handicapping factors in your selection process.

You might, for example, eliminate all of the following horses before applying the Performance Ratings:

1. Maidens (horses which have never won) racing against previous winners.
2. Females racing against males.
3. Horses, whose top races were run at a minor track, racing at a major track today.

Each of these elimination steps could have secured some high-priced *PRL* winners not included in our total of 1,218 wins. But it also would have eliminated many of the higher-priced horses which did qualify. Sy's Theme $119.60 (Example 6) was in the female vs. male category (No. 2); while Pawn $187.60 (Example 9) was moving from Northampton Fair–a minor track–to Lincoln Downs. These are just two examples.

Another possibility is to use one or more of the primary handicapping factors–such as class, form, speed and consistency–in pointing out a final play. Your selection, with this procedure, might be the highest-rated horse which meets certain form, class or speed requirements. Needless to say, this would greatly lower the average payoff.

Carrying this idea one step further, you could check-mark every qualified horse receiving one or more Performance points and make your selection from this group based on your own personal preference or your ability to handicap the contenders.

These alternatives raise the age-old question: which is better–handicapping or system play? We believe the question is academic.

The term "system" has become a dirty word for many players because it somehow suggests that the racegoer is not using his powers of judgment. But what difference does it really make whether we handicap a race systematically or rely on a system which is based on sound handicapping principles?

Too many self-styled handicappers rely on nothing more than specific angles in choosing their selections; result–they wind up juggling too many variables and thereby get caught in the switches.

OTHER POSSIBILITIES

We have stressed at all times that *Pro Rated Longshots* is a longshot system. This is equally true of the alternative Date Factors in the Intermediate Plan and the alternative Performance Ratings and Price Factors in the Advanced Plan.

There is no reason, however, why this basic approach could not be modified to secure winners at all prices.

While there are many ways to do this, two possibilities come to mind:

1. Eliminate all horses not earning a minimum rating score, such as 5, 10 or 15 points.
2. Change the Preliminary Elimination Rules so that horses which finished in the money (first, second, third) in their top race are playable.

By combining these two changes, the average payoff could be moved still lower. It is evident that any of these steps would require dropping the minimum 5-to-1 odds requirement unless you were interested only in a spot-play approach with very few selections.[22]

This completes the Advanced Plan. You are free, of course, to add your own refinements or create new and different rating plans.

However, we caution you once again to proceed with your plays in an orderly manner and thereby not get caught in the switches.

CONCLUSION

Since the accompanying text and the lists of winners which follow do not mention losers, you must not conclude that *Pro Rated Longshots* gets winners only—nothing could be further from the truth.

When realizing an average payoff of about $26, you can

play 10 losers for every winner and still come out with a flat-bet profit of more than 15 percent.

Also we have not dwelt on the winners "that got away" but this, too, is inevitable when stressing the longshot approach of *PRL*.

As just one example, consider what happened at Pimlico on April 18, 1974. The Basic Plan of *PRL* selected Rig A Jig $109.60 as a top-rated Step 1 2 play in the eighth race. In the very next event, another tremendous winner—Ramblin Reply $65.40—was eliminated because 7-1 April Storm beat him out by the narrow margin of 12 Performance Points to 10.

Although Ramblin Reply could have been made by both the Top-Two-Rated and Proportional Odds Price Factors, he was not a selection according to the simpler rules of the Basic Plan.

And in the sixth race, another top-rated winner—Sirloin Tip $20.00—was eliminated by the Price Factor because she was only 4-1 on the morning line of the *Daily Racing Form*.

PRL thereby missed the chance to snag one of its most notable triple wins in the past two years.

Such things are bound to happen, and we can only advise you to look to future plays, rather than the past, confident in the knowledge that *PRL* will always continue to get its share of profitable, high-priced payoffs.

Notes

1. *Page 15, line 7:* "Overlay"—a bet which gives the player sufficient percentage edge to overcome the track's takeout (take and breakage). If a horse figures to be 2-1 on its record but goes postward at 8-1 because it was overlooked in the betting, it is an overlay.

2. *Page 15, line 33:* "Chalk player"—one who bets on favorites.

3. *Page 16, line 25:* "Take"—commission deducted from mutuel pools (before breakage) which is shared by track and state. At most tracks it ranges from 15 percent to 18 percent.

4. *Page 16, line 33:* When a track breaks to the nickel, it keeps all pennies over 10-cent multiples (for example, the bettor receives $5.90 on a $5.98 winning ticket). Where a track breaks to the dime it retains all pennies over 20-cent multiples (for example, the bettor gets $5.80 on a $5.98 winning ticket). Most tracks break to the dime today.

5. *Page 20, line 2:* It beat 17 out of 24 tracks for one month using either the Step 1, Step 2, or Step 3 Date Rules. (See Part II, The Intermediate Plan.) This is based on a play in every race for Step 1 horses and a lesser number of pro rated plays for Step 2 and 3 horses.

6. *Page 20, line 29:* A more recent comparison, covering all of 1973, shows that *PRL* with 1,226 wins exceeded the combined total of System A (512 winners) and System B (680 winners) by 34 wins.

7. *Page 21, line 5:* All of these winners were selected by the Basic Plan of *PRL*. (See Part II, The Intermediate Plan).

8. *Page 24, line 1:* "Call"—an abbreviation for "point of call." It is a partway point in the race where the chartcaller calls the running position of each horse to his assistant. There are generally four calls in the race, corresponding roughly to quarter point, halfway point, beginning of the stretch (or straightaway) and finish.

9. *Page 24, line 6:* "Running forwardly"—a synonym for front-runner, or horse which leads or is close to the leader at every stage of the race.

10. *Page 27, line 27.* A horse which is moved higher in finishing position (i.e., second to first) because another horse is disqualified; moved lower in finishing position (i.e., first to second) because he is disqualified; or later disqualified from purse money because of being illegally drugged or other reasons. (This latter occurrence only affects purse money to owners, not payoffs to the bettors).

11. *Page 28, line 18:* "Running line"—the horse's running positions (superior numbers) and beaten-length margins (inferior numbers) at the four calls of the horse's most recent races. Most past performances show this information for the past ten races.

12. *Page 28, line 28:* There are actually six superior numbers in the running line, the first two numbers representing the horse's post position and its running position at the "break" or start of the race. These two left-hand numbers are easily distinguished from the four right-hand calls because they have no inferior numbers, i.e.:

$$1 \ 2 \ 3^2 \ 3^3 \ 5^5 \ 8^{10}$$

13. *Page 33, line 8:* In our survey we combined closing tote odds appearing in the result charts of the *Morning Telegraph* and *Daily Racing Form* with the morning lines in these papers. While this is permissible for research *after* the race, it is not recommended when betting *before* the race. (When at the track use the toteboard morning line or track program.)

14. *Page 52, line 31.* Two others which qualified only on the minimum date rules were Tartan John $108.20 and Linden Way $180.40, both of which won May 18.

15. *Page 54, line 23:* Bee Bee Bee (Example 4) and Pawn (Example 9) were also triple-top-rated winners as we explain below.

16. *Page 55, line 23:* A "spot play" is a system or approach which averages very few plays—perhaps two or three per day at the most.

17. *Page 56, line 9:* We never bet a supplemental (non-top-rated) horse where the situation is reversed (for example, a Step 1 horse with a lower Performance Rating than a Step 2, or a Step 2 horse rated lower than a Step 3). All Step 1 horses must be top-rated to qualify for play.

18. *Page 56, line 21:* When we speak of Step 2 and Step 3 horses we only consider the highest-rated horse in the race which meets these respective date requirements. We do not play just any Step 2 or Step 3 horse.

19. *Page 56, line 29:* If Horse B had not been in the example race above, then Horse C would have been the highest-rated horse after Horse A (who only qualified on the minimum date rule). Since Horse C qualified on both the moderate and the restrictive date rules he would have been a Step 2 3 play.

20. *Page 57, line 1:* The same problem arises when two horses tie for the top Performance Rating (see Supplement 1 covering rating ties).

21. *Page 68, line 3:* A more meaningful evaluation of the Equal Call and Outer Call Ratings is provided by this comparison of Step 1 (top-rated) winners during all of 1973 covering the same tracks as the 1972 survey:

Number of Winners	\$ *Payoff Range*					*Total*
Picked Exclusively by:	*12-20*	*20-30*	*30-50*	*50-100*	*100-Up*	*Winners*
Equal Call Rating	80	45	41	18	3	187
Outer Call Rating	80	43	26	11	4	164

This shows that the results are almost identical for the payoffs of $12 to $30, but that the Equal Call Rating has a decided edge in the higher payoff brackets.

22. *Page 81, line 19:* Another possibility, in just the opposite direction, is to bet the two horses with the highest *PRL* Performance Ratings in races with exacta or perfecta wagering. See the discussion of this subject in Supplement 1, Rating Ties.

Supplement 1

The remarkable consistency of winners in all price brackets when using *Pro Rated Longshots* is dramatically confirmed by this comparison of 1972 and 1973 results:

	Winners*	$12-$20	$20-$30	$30-$50	$50-$100	$100 & Up
1972	1,218	608	326	181	81	17
1973	1,226	586	336	199	86	16

*Includes five dead-heats for first place in 1972 and three ties for first in 1973.

This is about as consistent as you can get—especially when dealing with supposedly inconsistent longshots. What's more, the greater number of wins in the latter year was spread over fewer racing days than in 1972; and the percentage of winners paying more than $20 rose from just below 50 percent to 52 percent.

Another significant comparison of the two years is shown by the following:

	1972	1973
Top-rated Winners (Basic Plan)	937	952
Supplemental Winners (Intermediate Plan)	281	274

Here again the 1973 results not only equaled but surpassed those of 1972; also the ratio of top-rated to supplemental winners rose from 3.3 to 3.5.

SPECIFIC HIGHLIGHTS

The year 1973 has been called the "Year of Secretariat," a reference to one of the most famous racehorses of all time. Secretariat not only swept the Triple Crown (Kentucky Derby, Preakness, Belmont Stakes) for the first time since 1948 but was unanimously voted horse of the year in December, 1973.

PRL, which had pinpointed the surprise winner of the Preakness in 1972 (when Bee Bee Bee defeated Secretariat's stablemate, Riva Ridge), produced a still greater upset when it picked this winner in Belmont Park's Woodward Stakes on September 29:

PROVE OUT $34.40

Winning this race by 4½ lengths, Prove Out defeated the overwhelming favorite, Secretariat, who had been bet down to only 3-10 by the overflow Saturday crowd.

Prove Out was a standout *PRL* selection with a very high Performance Rating of 23 points; the only other qualifier in the race had just four points.

Its ability to snag the winners of feature races had been confirmed on March 31, 1973, when these *PRL* selections won important stakes races on the same day:

LEO'S PISCES $109.80
ROYAL AND REGAL . . . . $ 15.20

Leo's Pisces won the climactic Louisiana Derby at Fair Grounds while Royal and Regal captured Gulfstream's richest race—the Florida Derby.

Embellishing the Florida win was the fact that *PRL* had picked this blockbuster earlier on the same day at Gulfstream Park:

MERISIER $100.40

The top payoff for the year, however, was this bombshell snagged at Hialeah Park on February 9:

FUN CO K. $216.20

Some other winners topping the $100 level in 1973 included:

Feb.9, Santa Anita
SILVER SALUTE $127.00
July. 26, Hawthorne
COLOR ME NEW $101.20
Sept. 5, Sportsman's Park
VALIANT AND WISE $113.20

Pro Rated Longshots also pinpointed this spectacular multiple win at Chicago's Arlington Park on June 21:

WALL STREET MIDGE . . . . $ 19.20
JERSEY JET . . . . $ 14.80
POKACHIEF . . . . $ 14.20
PRINCE TERRELL . . . . $ 59.80

On March 5 at Aqueduct, *PRL* had these winners on the same card:

SERGEANT MAJOR . . . . $ 31.40
NEELROD . . . . $ 38.80
THE YANKEE SQUIRE . . . . $ 15.60

A more impressive triple, pricewise, was this collection of *PRL* winners at Liberty Bell on August 31:

GONE ASHORE . . . . $ 28.80
SASSY SATAN . . . . $ 51.40
GALLANT MEMORY . . . . $ 20.60

And at Lincoln Downs on February 7, it had already snagged these payoffs:

NOT NEEDED . . . . $ 40.00
BROTHER EMMANUEL . . . . . . $ 15.60
FIFTY COINS . . . . $ 71.80

Here are some of the noteworthy double wins achieved by *PRL* during the same year:

Jan. 12, Calder Race Course
        SON OF BRICK $129.80
        CAREER GIRL II . . . . $ 37.00

Feb. 14, Santa Anita
        LASTING HONOUR . . . . $ 46.60
        WINTER KISS . . . . $ 43.00

Apr. 27, Gulfstream Park
        PROHIBIDO . . . . $ 34.40
        GOODBYE JUANITA . . . . $ 56.40

Aug. 17, Monmouth Park
        DEACON DON . . . . $ 60.80
        TRADER ED . . . . $ 37.60

Sept. 20, Bowie
        KALIMERA . . . . $ 62.00
        BIG VIN . . . . $ 52.20

Oct. 8, Sportsman's Park
        HEY HURRY . . . . $ 90.40
        HANNAH'S JR. . . . . $ 51.00

Dec. 25, Calder Race Course
        IT SPOTTY . . . . $ 50.60
        VILLAGE RAMP . . . . $ 49.40

Dec. 31, Narragansett Park
        MOKETU . . . . $ 64.00
        NAUSSETT LIGHT . . . . $ 50.60

On December 14, *Pro Rated Longshots* picked this winner in the first race at Calder Race Course:

        PRETTY CHIPPER . . . . $ 93.60

Pretty Chipper was the first half of Calder's record-breaking daily double payoff of $7,907.80. (We have already shown how *PRL* wholly or partly sparked the record-breaking daily doubles at Gulfstream Park and Lincoln Downs in 1972.)

Winners at Other Tracks

From October 1 to November 10 of 1973, *PRL* was spot-checked at several major tracks not covered in the 1972 and 1973 surveys. These included Churchill Downs and Keeneland in Kentucky; Detroit Race Course; Thistledown in Ohio; and Bay Meadows in California.

Topping the list of its winners was this string of boxcar payoffs on three successive racing days at Thistledown:

Oct. 5	BUSH BANDIT	$ 91.40
Oct. 6	MALTANA	$134.80
Oct. 8	GOLDEN GLADIATOR	$117.20

Even assuming one play in every race, and no other *PRL* winners during the three-day period, the percentage of profit on $2 flat win bets (10 races per day) amounted to 472 percent!

Other top-rated winners picked by the Basic Plan of *PRL* at these tracks included:

Oct 4, Detroit
    TABCO $101.60

Oct. 15, Detroit
    COMMODITY MARKET . . . . . . $ 61.60

Oct. 17, Thistledown
    PARI-NOBLE . . . . $ 85.00

Oct. 17, Keeneland
    MODEST MORN . . . . $ 70.60

Oct. 20, Detroit
    DRAFT'S GIN . . . . $ 55.20

Oct. 29, Detroit
    CHACHOULA . . . . $ 99.60

Nov. 2, Detroit
    UNO TROUBLE . . . . $ 52.00

Nov. 7, Churchill Downs
    ROMAN SUNUP $129.80

Nov. 10, Bay Meadows
    MUCH . . . . $ 54.80
    CAVERN . . . . $ 25.40

None of these winners is included in the above comparison of 1972 and 1973 *PRL* winners.

1974 Winning Spree

On February 21, 1974, *PRL* had these winners at the only major tracks with past performance records in the Eastern *Daily Racing Form* for that day:

Garden State:
      PASQUA CUNIGLIOLA . . . . $ 18.40
      POSITIVE PETE . . . . $ 47.20

Bowie:
      FEAR A BIT $116.60

Gulfstream Park:
      LORD ARLEN   . . . . $ 64.80
      SASSY CYANE   . . . . $ 42.20

All of the winners listed in this 1973-1974 supplement were top-rated selections picked by the Basic Play of *PRL*.

Supplement 2

RATING TIES

During the survey year, 101 of the 1,218 *PRL* winners were involved in ties for the top Performance Rating. (See Example 10).

In the few instances where more than two horses tied for the top rating, we played the two horses with the highest toteboard odds. In all other cases, we played both horses.

Our records show that the 101 winners combined for a total win payoff of $3,053.20. The average payoff was $30.23, considerably higher than the $26 figure for all 1,218 winners.

By playing only the horse with the highest odds, instead of both horses, we would have settled for only 33 winners, although the total return on these winners was slightly more than on the 64 horses which won at lower odds.

Here is the actual breakdown:

ANALYSIS OF 101 WINNERS
INVOLVED IN RATING TIES

	No. of Wins	Total Return	Ave. Payoff
Horse at Higher Odds	33	$1,558.80	$47.24
Horse at Lower Odds	64	$1,425.80	$22.28
Combined Total:	97	$2,984.60	$30.23

Note: There were four races where both horses went postward at the same toteboard odds or the odds on the losing horse were not available. Their combined payoffs of $68.60 were excluded from the total-return figure in the table above.

It might appear from the above that the best alternative is to play the horse at the highest odds only, since a greater return was achieved on a smaller total investment.

However, since we accept one horse for play at minimum odds of 5-1, we can logically play two horses in the same race provided the average payoff is 11-1 ($24) or greater, since the latter figure also provides a 5-1 return on our money. (In other words $24 minus $4 = $20; $20 = 5 x $4).

Also, by playing the horse with the highest odds only, we still would have missed such winners as False Impression $63.00 (the other horse was 45-1), No No Fool $80.00 (the other horse was 95-1), and Douvrendelle $50.20 (the other horse was 83-1).

Here is another good argument for playing both horses when they tie for the top Performance Rating:

Pro Rated Longshots managed to pick three winning exactas or perfectas (involving the two horses tied with top Performance Ratings) though only 42 of the 101 races had exacta or perfecta wagering.

Note: In exactas or perfectas the bettor must pick the first two horses in the exact order of finish, which requires two bets (A to win, B to place; B to win, A to place). The payoffs were as follows:

May 5,	Aqu	8	Exacta	$299.60
May 12,	Aqu	8	Exacta	267.00
July 14,	AP	3	Perfecta	116.20
	Total:			$682.80

The payoffs on the winning exactas and perfectas not only exceeded the 42 exacta/perfecta wagers but also the 101 extra $2 bets entailed by playing two horses in a race.

Here is the total outlay for playing one extra horse in 101 races plus the exacta or perfecta bets:

101 extra win bets @ $2	$202.00
42 exactas/perfectas @ $4	168.00
Total:	$370.00

The total return on the winning exactas and perfectas provided a net profit of $312.80 on a $2 flat-bet basis ($682.80 returned minus $370.00 wagered), a profit yield of 84.5 percent.

These arguments for playing two horses in the same race apply with equal force to the conflict between Step 1 and Step 2 plays (discussed in the Intermediate Plan) and can even be applied to top-rated and second-rated *PRL* selections.

EXPLANATION OF SYMBOLS

Top-rated horse qualifies on:

Minimum date rule only.	1
Minimum and Moderate date rules.	1 2
Minimum, moderate, and restrictive date rules.	1 2 3

(All Step 1 winners are top-rated horses.)

Supplemental (non-top-rated) horse qualifies on:

Moderate date rule, and top-rated horse qualifies on minimum date rule only.	2
Moderate and restrictive date rules, and top-rated horse qualifies on minimum date rule only.	2 3
Restrictive date rule, and top-rated horse (or higher-rated horse) qualifies on minimum and moderate date rules.	3

(Horses qualifying on special Step 3 spot play
are identified as follows — 3*.)

Appendix 1—Basic and Intermediate Plan Winners

> Basic Plan includes Step 1, Step 1 2 (Double-Top-Rated) and Step 1 2 3 (Triple-Top-Rated) winners.
>
> Intermediate Plan includes Step 2, Step 3, and Step 2 3 winners.

Appendix 2—Advanced Plan Winners

> Picked by Outer Call Performance Rating.

Appendix 3—Advanced Plan Winners

> Picked by Top-Two-Rated Price Factor.
>
> *Note:* Winners appearing in Appendix 2 and in Appendix 3 are additional winners not picked by the Standard or Intermediate Plans (Appendix 1).

Other Symbols

† 4/8 Aqu 2—These horses coupled as an entry had the two highest Performance Ratings.

*5/1 Aqu 8, 5/12 Aqu 8, 7/14 AP 3—The two horses which tied with the highest Performance Ratings ran one-two and created winning exacta or prefecta payoffs.

T 1/12 SA 5, 8/12 Lib 1, 9/14 LD 8, 9/11 Rkm 2, 11/1 Suf 3—Horse finished in tie (dead-heat) for first place.

#Appendix 2— indicates horses were supplemental, but not top-rated, winners of the Equal Call Rating Plan.

Track Abbreviations

Ap	Arlington Park (Ill.)	LD	Lincoln Downs (R.I.)
Aqu	Aqueduct (N.Y.)	Lib	Liberty Bell (Pa.)
Atl	Atlantic City (N.J.)	Lrl	Laurel (Md.)
Bel	Belmont Park (N.Y.)	Mth	Monmouth Park (N.J.)
Bow	Bowie (Md.)	Nar	Narragansett (R.I.)
Crc	Calder Race Course (Fla.)	Pim	Pimlico (Md.)
Del	Delaware Park (Del.)	Rkm	Rockingham Park (N.H.)
FG	Fair Grounds (La.)	SA	Santa Anita (Cal.)

GP	Gulfstream Park (Fla.)	Sar	Saratoga (N.Y.)
GS	Garden State (N.J.)	Spt	Sportsman's Park (Ill.)
Haw	Hawthorne (Ill.)	Suf	Suffolk Downs (Mass.)
Hia	Hialeah Park (Fla.)	TrP	Tropical Park (Fla.)

Note: Calder Race Course has replaced Tropical Park in the Florida major winter-track circuit.

Definitions

Colt—entire male to and including four years of age.

Filly—female to and including four years of age.

Gelding—castrated male horse.

Horse—entire male five years old or older.

Mare—female five years old or older.

Types of Races

Stakes—feature races for classiest horses.

Handicaps—feature races for classy horses assigned specific weights by the track handicapper.

Allowances—intermediate races for horses which can not be claimed; sometimes used as preps for feature races.

Claiming races—for cheaper horses which can be claimed at stated prices by other owners.

Maiden races—for horses which have never won (maiden special weights for classier maidens, maiden claimers for cheaper maidens).

Other Terms

Entry—two or more horses which run for same owner or trainer coupled as one betting unit.

Field—two or more horses running as one betting unit because the field size exceeds maximum number of betting units, which can be shown on the toteboard. At most tracks, it is 12; at some, it is 10.

Appendix 1

LIST OF WINNERS IN 1972

Jan. 1

Bow	2	Miss Winkle	25.80	1	2	3
TrP	5	Hopeful Road	16.60			3*
Nar	6	Fur Trim	26.80			3*
FG	4	Gyro Gem	12.40	1		
	6	Doll Market	13.40	1	2	

Jan. 3

Bow	6	Whiskey Romeo	13.40	1	2	3
TrP	5	Highland Lady	26.40	1	2	
Nar	6	Bacchanal	22.20	1	2	3
FG	4	Arian Star	33.60	1	2	

Jan. 4

Lib	2	Lady Carene	27.60		2	
TrP	2	Peskitality	20.60	1	2	
	3	Tune Up Time	29.60	1	2	3
Nar	6	Wagay	16.60			3
FG	1	Molloqua	43.80		2	
	5	American Lass	20.80		2	

Jan. 5

Lib	1	Prince Presto	18.40	1	2	
Bow	1	Sky Flight	14.40	1	2	
	5	King Johns Sun	22.40		2	3
TrP	6	Mio Mine	12.60	1	2	

Tr P	7	Wild Rivers	22.80	1	
FG	7	Gaby Lee	26.40	1	
SA	2	Two Exact	26.00	1	

Jan. 6

Lib	2	Run It Up	12.80	1 2	
Bow	7	Early	13.80	1 2	
TrP	6	Polar Miss	17.60		3*
Nar	4	Prissis Pebble	31.40	1 2	

Jan. 7

Lib	2	Andy Al	12.80	1 2	
Bow	7	Thunderhorn	13.00	1 2 3	
	9	Little Red Rocket	15.20	1	
Nar	5	Pots Lag	20.60	1 2 3	

Jan. 8

Lib	5	Mr. Poverty	15.40	1 2 3	
Bow	2	Contented Clown	21.20		3*
	3	Delightful Squaw	17.00	1 2	
TrP	7	Bold Pep	14.60	1	
FG	2	Tuinadek	15.00	2	
	10	Janann	12.40	1	

Jan. 10

Bow	2	Mydarlindawter	19.00		3
	3	Bens Sparkler	12.80	1 2	
Nar	5	Hahn Road	14.00	1 2	

Jan. 11

Lib	1	Cold Draft	20.60	1 2	
TrP	6	Princess Nashima	37.00	1 2	
SA	2	Sir Larry Jay	16.60	1 2	

Jan. 12

Bow	2	All the Luck	18.60	1 2	
TrP	6	Wonderous Sky	23.80		3
FG	5	Eternal Prince	18.60		3
SA	5	Winter War (13-1)	14.60^T	1	

Jan. 13

Lib	5	To a Skylark	12.20			3
FG	2	Cheniere Pass	14.00	1	2	3
	7	Devils Dyke	22.40	1	2	3
SA	8	Tradesman	13.20	1		

Jan. 14

Lib	7	Petrous	36.00	1	2	3
TrP	2	Bossy	12.80	1		
	9	Knight Counter	15.20	1	2	

Jan. 15

Bow	2	White Spring	29.60	1	2	
TrP	10	Better B. Dan	34.60			3
Nar	2	Calhoun Special	12.00	1	2	
FG	3	Clearance	25.20	1	2	3
	4	First and Goal	23.40	1		
SA	5	Nashua Road	16.80	1	2	

Jan. 18

Lib	1	Activism	16.60	1	2	
	2	Bull Of The Woods	30.40	1	2	3

Daily double 310.00

Bow	5	Braddock's Road	48.40	1	2	3
GP	3	Gum Ball	13.00	1	2	

Jan. 19

Lib	2	Tudor Tune	15.20	1	2	
	4	Ft. King	49.20		2	
	9	Market Tour	17.40	1		
Bow	9	Maleeny	44.00	1		
GP	1	Croquet Game	18.80	1	2	3
Nar	3	Road Actress	16.80		2	
FG	9	Blondheim	13.20	1		

Jan. 20

Lib	6	A Lucky Day	29.80	1	2	
Nar	2	Flying Red Robin	15.20	1		

Jan. 21

Lib	9	Ermine Beauty	14.80	2
Bow	6	Patrol Prince	19.00	1 2
GP	6	Aromanite	26.80	1 2
	10	Gloriosky	15.20	2
Nar	2	Ear Ring	14.80	1 2
	8	Ce Ce's Pride	37.00	1 2
	9	Gee Linda	14.60	1 2 3
FG	2	Chic's Link	27.80	1 2

Jan. 22

Na	7	Cantilever	46.40	3*
SA	6	Aggressively	24.80	2

Jan. 24

Lib	7	King's Demand	17.80	1 2
	9	Small Group	25.40	1 2

Jan. 25

Lib	3	Itty Bitty Bride	44.00	1 2
Bow	4	More Or Less	22.60	1
Nar	5	Three Corners	24.20	1

Jan. 26

GP	1	Noble Duel	230.40	1 2
	2	Sy's Theme	119.60	1

Daily double 6,683.60

Na1	9	Fire and Sword	29.60	3*
FG	4	Full Steam Ahead	15.60	1 2 3
	6	Sheep's Clothing	14.80	1 2 3

Jan. 27

Bow	7	Vava	20.80	3
	9	Count Porter	59.80	1 2
GP	2	Bio Devil	12.60	3
Nar	2	Calcasieu Pass	18.40	3*
SA	9	Jack Teel	21.00	1 2

Jan. 28

Bow	9	Ground Mist	40.40				3*
Nar	1	Ricorullah	59.60	1	2	3	
	8	Duke Of Winloc	25.80	1	2		
FG	5	Kopes Angel	20.20	1	2	3	
	7	Satin Lark	25.80		2		
SA	8	Fair Test	18.80	1	2	3	
	9	Party Suit	16.80	1			

Jan. 29

Lib	7	Oak Spring	17.20	1	2		
FG	2	Tempermental Tom	51.20				3*
	5	Red Clark	23.00	1	2		

Jan. 31

Bow	4	Mad Kick	14.00	1		
	6	Stage Trust (entry)	24.60			3
Nar	2	Baybush	17.80	1	2	3
	4	Rejjy	13.00			3
FG	1	Bated Cloud	17.40	1	2	3
	6	Taul Hill	24.80		2	3

Feb. 1

Lib	6	Edisto	16.60	1	2		
Bow	3	Joy Smoke	12.40	1	2		
GP	5	Kauaian	17.80				3*
SA	2	Miss Gummo	20.00	1	2		

Feb. 2

Lib	2	Who Gets It	14.40			3
	8	Say Percy	14.00	1		
GP	1	Barbs Fella	27.60		2	
	2	Frank Lynch	14.00	1	2	
Daily double 253.20						
	5	Note Notice	14.20	1	2	
FG	6	Little Dancer	20.40	1	2	3
SA	2	Big Red Bird	169.40		2	
	3	Prime Prince	17.40	1		

Feb. 3

Lib	5	Positive Pete	88.20			3
	7	Miami Maid	14.00	1	2	
Bow	4	Egalite	20.00	1	2	
	9	Jim's Hat	12.40			3
FG	1	Table's Girl	21.40			3
	5	Mack's Legacy	12.20			3

Feb. 4

Lib	8	Brass Duc	14.80	1	2	
GP	8	Search The Farm	37.40	1		
Nar	1	Hemprince	15.20		2	3
FG	2	Hawleys Pet	17.60	1	2	
SA	2	Winged Steed	12.40		2	
	6	The Pie Host	20.40	1		

Feb. 5

Bow	9	Parire	146.00	1		
GP	1	Oxbridge	16.00	1		
FG	2	Beribot	14.40	1	2	
SA	1	Dr. Hark	19.20	1		

Feb. 7

Bow	9	Cafir II	39.40	1	2	3
FG	2	Distant Music	13.00	1	2	3

Feb. 8

SA	5	To Market Jr.	27.00	1	2	

Feb. 9

FG	6	Mountain Crest	22.80	1	2	3
	9	Edomite	29.00	1	2	
SA	4	Oh Lucky Day	15.20	1	2	
	9	Luckiest of All	13.00	1	2	

Feb. 10

Bow	5	Double Riddle	12.60		2	3

Bow	6	Sam Bolero	12.40	1	2	
GP	4	Lyrs Poker	16.20		2	3
	9	Pajara	93.80			3*
Nar	1	Lucky Monarch	15.40			3
	2	Midget Widget	15.60	1	2	
(Daily double 128.60)						
SA	5	Calgary Miss	44.40		2	

Feb. 11

Bow	5	Dacquare	41.80	1	2	
	8	Crimson Saber	15.00	1	2	
Nar	2	Matt Squiet	20.00	1	2	3

Feb. 12

Bow	6	Musical Sadie	12.00	1	2	3
	7	Sew To Bed	47.00	1	2	3
GP	7	Brick Passer	25.80	1	2	
Nar	2	Awendaw	41.60	1	2	3
FG	1	Sea Heiress	23.60	1		
	2	Tuxedo Junction	29.00	1	2	3
Daily double 278.00						

Feb. 14

Bow	5	Watawopper	18.20		2	3
Nar	5	Colonel Tuleg	70.60	1	2	3
FG	6	Chaland Pass	15.20		2	

Feb. 15

Nar	7	Middle Fury	104.40	1	2	
FG	2	Ubique	49.60	1	2	
SA	7	A Lotta Laughs (entry)	20.40	1	2	

Feb. 16

Bow	8	Amber Hawk	14.00		2	
Nar	1	Sky Menace	44.20	1	2	3
	9	False Impression	63.00	1	2	

Feb. 17

Bow	4	Atlantic Breeze	30.60	1	2	3

GP	2	I Will Do It	12.60	1 2
Nar	3	Fast Foot	20.60	1 2

Feb. 18

Bow	1	Rythm	18.00	1
GP	7	Bo Hatch	86.60	3
FG	1	Ngoron Goron	16.40	3
	4	Gateway Girl	18.00	1 2

Feb. 19

GP	3	Majestic Isle	52.80	1 2 3
FG	10	Fear A Bit	18.40	1 2 3

Feb. 22

Bow	2	Exclusive Belmont	21.20	1 2
GP	2	Stool Pigeon	22.60	1

Feb. 23

Bow	5	Crimsonade	25.40	1
	7	Jack The Sailor	56.60	1
	8	Son O'Fancy	18.40	1 2 3
GP	6	Petrous	49.40	3
FG	6	Dark Stone	18.20	1

Feb. 24

GP	2	Au Gratin	18.40	3
	5	Nancy Wynne	16.40	1 2
	8	Search The Farm	19.60	1 2 3
Nar	2	Genie's Prince	15.00	3
FG	6	Polynesian Flame	23.40	3*

Feb. 25

Bow	1	Double Levee	24.20	1 2
GP	5	De Soto Queen	17.20	1 2
	8	Hillaine	27.80	1 2
Nar	4	Mr. J.V.F.C.	115.40	3*
FG	1	Kenai	27.60	1 2
	10	Cinder I.	22.60	1 2 3

Feb. 26

GP	1	Double Dillie Du	21.40	1	
	3	Joie de Vivre	62.20		3
	5	Break Or Make	40.40	1 2 3
FG	7	Buddy Friedrichs	19.60	1	

Feb. 28

Bow	2	Jay's Honor	17.40	1	
GP	4	Evelyns Pride	29.80	1	
	8	We'll Call You	14.80	1 2	
FG	8	Royal Pussycat	18.00	1 2	

Feb. 29

FG	1	Traffic Stream	27.80	1

March 1

Bow	3	Jalbe	13.20	1 2	
	9	Gin Drinker	56.60	2	
GP	4	Florida Royal	15.20	1 2	
Nar	9	Rule of Reason	25.60	1 2 3

March 2

Aqu	1	Eye on the Sky	17.00	1 2 3
Bow	6	Lipp Mann	20.40		3*
GP	10	Smart Hit	58.80	1	
FG	7	Windon Tide	20.80	1 2 3
SA	8	Ace II	19.20	1 2 3

March 3

FG	5	Flying Martini	17.00	1 2

March 4

Nar	4	Mahitabul	19.20	2	
	10	Art's Voice	16.20	1 2 3
FG	2	Mad Irony	27.20	1 2	
	3	Whistling Coon	13.00	1 2	

March 6

FG	5	Straco	23.00	1 2

March 7

Bow	8	Enthusiastically	13.60	1	
Hia	4	Kings Brother	16.60		3
	8	Cast a Shadow	16.20	1 2	
Nar	3	Rougish Jester	24.60	1 2 3	

March 8

FG	1	Brenda Too	21.00	1 2	

March 9

Nar	2	Need A Mate	40.40	1	
FG	7	Slim Bim	12.20		3

March 10

Hia	6	Miss Fleet Ardan	37.00	1 2 3	

March 11

Bow	5	Samigo	33.80	1	
Hia	1	Picadilly Red	24.60	1 2	
	10	Water Gun	13.60	1 2	
Suf	4	Silver Buckle	17.60	1	
Nar	6	Andrian Nik	17.00		3

March 13

Pim	6	One More Pull	16.20	1 2	
	7	Sam Bolero	32.00	1 2	
Suf	1	Essi Dancer	134.00	1	
FG	4	Piroque	16.40		3

March 14

Nar	7	First Drill	17.60	1 2	
SA	8	Nor II	53.20		2

March 15

FG	4	City Lynx	17.20	1	
	5	Satan's Forest	13.00	1 2	

March 16

Pim	9	Gunner's Mate	14.20		3
FG	8	Believe You Me	32.60	1 2	

March 17

Hia	4	Lady's Knave	20.60	1 2

March 18

Hia	1	Brave Gypsy	62.00		2
	2	Miss Billy C.	25.20	1	
(Daily double 885.20)					
	4	Two Hopes	18.40	1	
	5	Iron Line	28.40	1 2	
Nar	3	Flogan	12.40	1 2	

March 20

Pim	1	Mary Lou T.	14.20	1 2
Hia	9	Queen Louie	22.80	1 2
Nar	8	Hail to Class	25.00	1

March 21

Pim	1	Rocky Rhythm	16.80	1 2

March 22

Hia	1	Victors Verse	20.20	1 2
Nar	6	Tax Talk	19.80	1 2 3

March 23

Pim	2	Tul Echo	22.00	2 3
	6	Mightly Bully	19.00	1 2
Suf	2	Olympia Mike	80.60	1 2
	6	Wee Hope	16.00	1 2
Nar	4	Queenly Lass	14.40	3
	7	Breezy Bev	14.40	1 2
FG	8	Rustle Up	21.00	1 2 3
	10	Terra Sands	12.20	1 2
SA	7	Northern Challenge	12.40	1 2 3

March 24

Hia	1	Tinderbox	17.20	1 2
	2	Mini Toga	14.00	1 2
	Daily double 93.40			
SA	1	Run for Your Money	53.20	3
	7	Traveling Fiddler	21.80	1

March 25

Aqu	5	Dan Patch	13.40	1
Pim	9	Templar	35.60	1 2
FG	1	Dr. Glen	54.80	1 2
	10	Cheniere Pass	38.20	1 2

March 27

Aqu	2	Exchange Place	12.40	1
Pim	1	Admiral Road	18.60	1 2 3
Nar	3	Rose Mary D.	35.20	1 2 3
	8	Maiden's Folly	16.60	2 3
FG	1	Hy Story	14.60	1 2 3

March 28

Pim	4	Old Scotch	23.20	1 2
	7	Pink Professor	24.60	1 2 3
Hia	8	Aloft	30.60	3

March 29

Pim	2	Reasonable Turn	12.80	1 2 3
	9	Nui Nui	15.20	1 2 3
Hia	2	Notwithstanding	15.00	1

March 30

Pim	1	Interstellar	16.00	1
Hia	5	Tupalou	138.00	1 2
Suf	7	Rockcastle Jr.	16.20	1 2
Nar	3	License To Steal	30.00	1 2 3
	6	Fleet Arrow	13.20	3

March 31

| Hia | 1 | Chargers Money | 21.80 | 1 2 |

April 1

Pim	1	Outrider	20.80	1
Hia	5	Topi	23.80	2 3
	8	Lionized	23.80	1
Suf	6	Crimson Victory	15.40	1

April 3

| Aqu | 8 | Dodeys Sky High | 39.60 | 1 2 |
| Suf | 2 | Fire Show | 32.20 | 1 2 3 |

April 4

| Pim | 8 | Carryin Fire | 22.60 | 1 2 |
| Nar | 7 | Andrian Nik | 26.80 | 1 2 3 |

April 5

Aqu	6	Wonderous Sky	25.00	1
Hia	9	Seminole Joe	56.20	1 2
Nar	2	Chester Martini	16.00	1 2
	5	Waxeys Pride	15.20	1 2 3
	6	Sloop	43.00	1 2 3
	7	Marching Yil	12.60	3

April 6

Aqu	8	La Bertha	16.60	1
Pim	1	Last Noble	19.20	1
Hia	5	Naturally Tops	15.80	1 2
	8	Called Red	21.20	1

April 7

Hia	7	Holme Early (entry)	40.00	1 2
SA	7	Procne	23.60	1 2
	8	Violonor	15.80	1 2

April 8

| Aqu | 2† | Eye On The Sky | 31.60 | 1 2 |
| | | Eagles Spring (entry) | 31.60 | 1 2 |

Hia	5	County Judge	22.00	1 2	
SA	5	Derringer	14.00	1 2	
	8	Practicante	19.80	1	

April 10

Aqu	7	Mindy Malone	48.40	1	
Nar	9	Bethson	43.00		3

April 11

Pim	2	Monroes Hobo	12.20	1	
	5	Mr. Buttnell	14.60	2 3	
	9	Texas Girl	35.60	1	
Nar	5	Shannon Babe	18.20	2 3	
	9	Start Over Again	37.80	1 2 3	

April 12

Aqu	2	Tudor Tune	69.20	1	
Hia	4	Ribatejo	12.60		3
Suf	4	Nodlac	14.40	1 2 3	
Nar	9	Macwonder	31.20	1 2 3	

April 13

Aqu	1	Grand Bonanza	14.20	1 2 3	
	3	Feminist	35.60	1 2	
Pim	2	Sebulea	41.60	1 2	
Hia	3	Goodbye Juanita	53.40	1 2 3	
Suf	6	Calhoun Toe	25.40	1 2 3	

April 14

Hia	6	Natogo	12.20		3

April 15

Aqu	6	Single Line	15.80	1	
Pim	7	Typhoon Tina	24.80	1	
Hia	5	Dr. C. Salk	13.80	1	
Nar	1	Pizzagalla	22.20		3
Suf	7	Certain Splendor	31.60	1 2	

April 17

| Pim | 6 | Killough | 44.00 | 1 2 3 |
| Nar | 8 | Cholly | 46.00 | 1 |

April 18

| Pim | 6 | Imapuncher | 13.20 | 3 |
| Haw | 2 | Ricks Beard | 21.40 | 1 |

April 19

| Nar | 3 | Billy's Blaze | 34.80 | 3* |
| | 9 | Tan Fantasy | 12.60 | 1 |

April 20

Hia	7	Mi Rebano	18.00	1 2
Nar	3	Murph's Umbrella	21.60	3
	6	Marching Yil	12.00	1 2 3
	9	First Ray	18.20	1 2 3
Haw	3	Another Cheiron	32.20	1 2

April 21

Hia	1	Short Temper	16.40	1 2
Nar	8	All Wound Up	28.00	1 2 3
	9	Aden G.	31.40	3*
Haw	2	Better Mood	12.80	2

April 22

Hia	2	First Score	13.00	1 2 3
	7	New Alibhai	12.00	1 2
	10	Papa Requested	17.40	1 2 3
Haw	5	Lostcreekprince	23.60	1 2

April 24

Aqu	4	Weigh Anchor	12.40	1 2 3
Pim	9	Private Times	30.80	1
Suf	1	Bu Bom	17.20	1 2 3
	2	Fancy Knave	12.60	1 2

Daily double 162.20

| | 4 | Phantoms Den | 23.20 | 1 |

April 25

Pim	8	Crimsonade	16.60	1 2	
Hia	3	La Vera G.	36.20	1 2	
Haw	1	Missouri Jester	74.00	1 2	
	4	Jr. Spectacular	41.20	2	

April 26

Aqu	7	Rule by Reason	19.00	1 2 3	
GS	8	Saturnina	29.60	1 2 3	
Pim	5	Thayer	16.40	1 2 3	
Nar	8	Loser's Delight	24.00	3*	

April 27

GS	8	Mr. Correlation	17.20	1
Haw	8	Dedicator	31.20	1 2

April 28

Aqu	6	Prime Prince	15.20	1

April 29

GS	4	Linstock	17.80	1	
Pim	3	Get Aboard	30.20		3
	7	Goodtobegone	19.20	1 2	
Nar	4	Yarak	15.00	1 2	
	9	Blue Lady Lark	35.80	1 2 3	
Hia	8	Whitsun	19.00	1 2	
Haw	3	Fastra Head	14.20	1 2	
	9	Lebanese Doctor	25.00	2 3	

May 1

Pim	4	Go Bet	25.00	1 2
Suf	2	Firm Denial	28.20	1 2 3
Haw	1	Lucky Pro	18.20	1

May 2

GS	3	Empress Mary	18.40	1
Pim	7	Proven Out	29.60	1 2

May 3

Aqu	8	The General	33.40	1 2	
Pim	1	April Formal	14.00	1 2 3	
Nar	2	Pokies Tip	22.60	1 2 3	
	3	Garde Rullah	28.40	1 2	
	5	Boulamite	26.00	1 2	

May 4

Aqu	1	First Cut	15.60	1 2 3	
	2	Reely Good	18.00	1 2	

Daily double 173.00

May 5

Aqu	8	*(Won For Nurse	38.40	1 2	
		(Clystalla	2nd 8-1	1 2	

Exacta 299.60

Pim	9	Smart Image	12.00	1 2	
Nar	1	Shemya	14.20	1 2	

May 6

GS	2	Old Grove	13.80	2	
	7	Dot Ed's Bluesky	12.60	1 2	
Pim	6	Three Letter	13.20	1	
Nar	1	Maid in Culpeper	14.60	1	

May 8

Pim	3	Bold Boot	18.20	1	

May 9

Pim	1	Cutie's Uncle	13.60	1	
	3	Hong Kong Lady	28.80		3
	4	Brave Maid	13.00	1	
	9	Light Airs	17.20	1 2	

May 10

Pim	4	Hidare Navy	15.60		3

May 11

GS	1	Lady Tea Tray	17.80	1	

GS	6	Gogethemoney	73.00	3*
Pim	4	Sebulea	12.40	1 2 3
Nar	7	Haluva Gal	17.40	3*
Suf	5	Partitime Pet	15.00	1 2 3
	9	Bottom to Top	23.20	1 2 3

May 12

Aqu	8	*(Romeo Lad	21.20	1 2
		(Scungagad	2nd 10-1	1 2
	Exacta 267.00			
Haw	8	Judge Tytus	12.60	1

May 13

Aqu	2	Tahoe Lake	37.60	2 3
Pim	1	Enforcer	22.40	1 2 3
Haw	2	Es Kup	19.60	1 2

`May 15

Bel	8	Tank	25.80	1 2 3
Pim	1	Artist's Pride	17.00	1 2 3
	4	Hidden Time	15.20	1 2 3
	9	Little Nassau	15.80	1
Haw	2	Rustys Brother	12.40	1 2 3
	4	Needle and Ball	18.80	1 2
	9	Amdor	27.20	2 3

May 16

Pim	9	Sword Swallower	12.20	3

May 17

Nar	2	Soleil II	17.80	3
Suf	5	O. Roger H.	16.20	1 2 3
	8	Just a Baker	14.00	1 2 3

May 18

Nar	8	Boswell Jr.	23.80	1 2 3
Suf	5	Star of Lebanon	14.60	1 2
	7	Tartan John	108.20	1
Haw	5	Bold Baron	14.80	1 2 3
	9	Linden Way	180.40	1

May 19

GS	5	Glider Girl	25.20	1 2	
Pim	5	Ambi Hula	36.00	2 3	
Nar	6	Quest for Oil	14.00	1 2 3	
	7	Ninfa's Joy	29.40	1	
	8	Marden	14.80	1 2 3	
Suf	9	Firm Denial	19.20	1 2 3	
Haw	1	Gay Laddie	26.00	1 2 3	

May 20

GS	2	Secret Advisor	21.60	3	
Pim	2	Rythm	24.40	1 2 3	
	8	Bee Bee Bee	39.40	1 2 3	
Nar	7	Nor Les	12.00	1 2 3	

May 22

GS	9	Cloudy Aire	12.60	1 2 3	
Pim	8	Native Wave	17.20	1	
Nar	2	Dottsie	14.00	1 2	

May 23

GS	7	Get Hep	24.20	3*	
Haw	6	Vapor Line	12.80	1 2 3	
	7	Rising Breeze	22.40	1 2	
	8	Peter Graff	19.80	1 2 3	

May 24

Bel	8	Big Spruce	19.40	1 2 3	
	9	Life Cycle	69.20	1 2	
GS	1	Not A Game	20.00	1	
	6	Aloft	16.40	1 2	
Nar	2	Drew's Tudora	54.00	1	

May 25

Bel	2	Bid For Me	61.40	1 2	
	8	Bill Boland	18.40	1 2 3	
Suf	4	Scootit	12.20	3*	

Nar	3	Genie's Prince	56.00	1 2 3
	5	Fleet Arrow	27.00	3

May 26

Pim	4	Mister Gunn	28.80	1 2 3
Nar	5	Bayou Teche	23.20	3
Haw	6	Bucket O'Suds	26.40	3

May 27

GS	3	Destined Ruler	23.00	3
Nar	6	Big Demon	19.40	1 2 3
	8	Dream Bar	20.00	2 3
Haw	5	Persian Art	15.00	1 2 3

May 28

Suf	1	Via Relic	18.60	1

May 29

GS	3	Leabu	22.40	1 2 3
	7	Hail Bolero	67.40	1 2
Suf	5	Wandering Reef	18.40	1
	9	Big M'shuba	15.00	1 2 3
Nar	8	Circus Flea	19.00	3
Haw	1	Singin Gyp	21.20	1 2

May 30

Bel	8	Invicta II	20.60	1 2
Pim	4	Ramekin	17.80	1 2

May 31

Lib	6	Last Triumph	64.60	1
Pim	4	Static Symbol	25.40	1 2 3
AP	3	Pre Shave	12.20	1 2 3
	5	Al Fortune	39.00	1 2 3

June 1

Bel	1	Excited Miss	12.60	1 2 3

Mth	2	Wise Policy	12.40	1 2
	6	Sunwise	15.20	1 2 3
Lib	2	Olos Blond	15.40	1 2 3
Suf	5	Pebbles Sister	55.00	1 2 3
AP	4	Out and Back	19.60	3

June 2

Bel	4	Lady Butterfly	17.20	1 2
	9	Money Destroyer	21.40	3
Mth	5	Day and Age	19.80	1 2 3
	7	Sui Generis	17.80	1 2
LD	2	Edys Mike	12.80	1 2 3
Suf	9	Skullduggery	15.20	1 2

June 3

| Lib | 3 | Accordingly | 25.00 | 1 2 3 |

June 4

| Suf | 9 | Press Gallery | 15.20 | 1 2 |

June 5

Mth	8	Escaped	35.40	2 3
Lib	3	Rock Zoe Chell	15.40	1 2 3
	7	Sharon Lyn	48.20	1 2
Suf	5	Pass Again	44.20	3*
LD	1	Fair Behaved	32.80	1
AP	5	Swifty Gal	64.00	1 2 3
	8	Gun Tune	14.00	1 2 3

June 6

Bel	1	Francois Premier	17.00	3
Mth	5	Different	14.20	1 2
Lib	7	Maharif	21.40	1 2
AP	4	Figurative	12.20	1 2
	9	Mr. Merger Maker	16.40	1 2

June 7

| Mth | 2 | Fond Charles | 13.00 | 1 2 |

Del	1	To The Starboard	17.60	1	2	3
Lib	1	Come Collect	23.20	1	2	3
	6	Kings Desire'	17.40	1	2	3

June 8

Bel	1	Dick D's Baby	18.00	1	2	3
	6	Nice Bonnet	14.20	1	2	
	7	Naleesa	13.80	1	2	
	9	Out of School	15.20	1	2	3
Mth	1	Almost Formal	21.20	1	2	
	6	Kindly K.	34.40	1		
	9	Glider Boy	24.00			3*
Del	8	Perpetual II	35.00	1		
Lib	2	Suspicious Manner	19.20	1	2	3

June 9

Bel	2	Rare Adventure	20.80		2	
	6	North Sea	18.00	1	2	
Mth	8	Replate	55.80	1	2	
Lib	5	Gypsy Rattler	23.20			3*
Suf	7	Rock Burner	22.20	1	2	

June 10

Bel	4	Wildcat Country	12.80	1	2	
	.	Native Royalty	32.00	1	2	
AP	7	Land Commander	30.20			3

June 11

Suf	4	Scootit	18.00		2	3

June 12

Bel	5	Chips of Straw	15.80		2	3
	6	Butter Fat	17.40	1		
LD	2	Holly Hope	17.40	1		

June 13

Mth	6	Brite Axtion	18.80	1		

June 14

Mth	2	Royal Cloak	16.40	1 2 3
	6	Misty Dash	29.20	1 2
Del	7	Interstellar	13.60	1 2
Suf	6	Ta Co Pet	13.00	1 2
AP	6	Global Hi	17.00	2

June 15

Bel	5	Nederboy	26.20	1 2
Mth	4	Hicksville	21.40	1 2
Del	6	Dont Lose	61.60	1 2 3
	9	Ice Center	18.20	1
AP	2	Double True	22.00	1 2 3
	4	Mystic Flight	27.20	1 2 3

June 16

| Mth | 5 | Prince Jerry | 40.40 | 1 2 |
| Suf | 7 | Big Sprint | 12.00 | 1 2 3 |

June 17

| AP | 1 | Crack the Whip | 30.80 | 1 2 3 |
| | 2 | Cysto | 29.20 | 2 |

Daily double 453.60

| | 8 | Lyrs Poker | 24.80 | 1 2 |

June 18

| Del | 6 | Gogethemoney | 18.20 | 1 2 |

June 19

| Lib | 1 | Seldom by Chance | 16.20 | 1 2 3 |
| AP | 9 | Mr. Colleoni | 19.20 | 3 |

June 20

| Aqu | 1 | Navy Blue Blood | 12.40 | 1 |
| Lib | 4 | Tedera | 17.00 | 1 2 |

June 21

| Lib | 5 | Red Brocade | 14.40 | 1 2 3 |
| AP | 5 | Aturnchorus | 12.40 | 1 2 3 |

June 22

Mth	3	Sailor George	18.40	1	2	
Lib	9	Pogestra	16.00	1	2	3
AP	9	Maxies Sis	20.00	1		

June 23

Mth	2	Mary's Sister	23.40			3
	8	Majestic Queen	14.80	1		
Del	5	Say It Isnt So	14.40	1		
AP	1	Hittmup	35.60	1		

June 24

Mth	9	Back to Peace	21.20	1		
Del	2	Little Corrie	26.80	1	2	3
	5	Lancers Rubyait	17.60			3*
Lib	3	Lady Carmella	14.80	1	2	
AP	6	Red Tamao	16.40	1		

June 25

Del	9	Gaines Mill	21.20	1	2	3

June 26

Aqu	8	Weigh Anchor	18.80	1	2	3
Mth	2	Third King	17.40	1	2	
Del	1	Crimson Tigre	18.00	1	2	
AP	6	Gal O Gem	19.20	1		

June 28

Aqu	6	Pago Queen	39.00	1		
	7	Towzie Tyke	16.40	1	2	
Del	7	Antigua Star	37.20		2	
Lib	9	Tomevy	25.00	1	2	
AP	7	Mr. Trio	67.80	1	2	3

June 29

Del	2	Pretty Witty	14.20	1	2	
	5	Static Symbol	14.00	1	2	3
Lib	3	Mesopotamia	13.20	1	2	
AP	4	Plum Branch	73.80	1	2	3

June 30

Aqu	5	Breezy Sovereign	48.40	3*
Lib	5	Charlies Loser	19.60	1 2
Suf	1	Delta Cepheus	18.40	1 2 3

July 1

Aqu	9	Chioini Special	12.20	1
Del	1	Open Draft	14.00	1 2
AP	4	Long Decision	13.00	1 2
	9	Escon	92.40	1 2

July 3

Aqu	4	Temperance Gal	39.20	1 2
Lib	6	Trenthor Star	12.80	3*
AP	7	Social Endeavour	36.80	1 2

July 4

Aqu	3	Foxie Liege	14.00	1
Del	2	Go To The Devil	17.20	1 2
	9	Merry Perry	12.20	1
Suf	1	Nashville Sun	12.40	3
AP	5	Polar Miss	18.40	2

July 5

Lib	9	Dr. De Bakey	12.80	1
LD	8	Khaled Celerity	36.60	1 2

July 6

Aqu	4	Running Doe	28.20	2
Mth	4	Timber Tavern	29.80	1 2 3

July 7

Aqu	3	Viborg	12.40	1 2 3
	6	Chartered Course	39.00	3*
Mth	4	Some More	16.40	1 2
Lib	4	Norther Park	20.00	1 2 3

July 8

Aqu	1	Zoom	14.00	1 2	
	7	Key To The Mint	12.40	1	
Del	9	Image of Yuma	12.20	1 2 3	
AP	1	Lady Babington	15.00	2	

July 9

Del	10	James Quillo	76.60	2	
Suf	2	Queenly Lass	25.40	1 2 3	
	4	Bottom to Top	33.20	1 2 3	
	9	Prince Solomon	23.00	1 2	

July 10

Aqu	4	Step Nicely	21.40	1	
	9	Harkville	12.60	1 2	
Mth	2	No Time For Games	30.80	1 2	
Lib	1	Apperception	39.40	3	
	7	Andy Al	28.00	1 2	
AP	3	Clifford R.	20.00	1 2	

July 11

Aqu	5	Roba Bella	15.40	1	
Lib	4	I'm Restless	21.20	1 2	

July 12

Aqu	8	Companion Way	45.60	1	
Del	7	Gunnysdeb	29.60	1	
Suf	1	Advertence	30.80	1 2 3	
	7	Aliqueen	28.40	2	

July 13

Mth	3	No Bikini Atoll	18.20	1	
Lib	2	Full Beam	14.20	1 2 3	

July 14

Aqu	2	Passen Mood	13.80	1 2 3	
Mth	3	Lady Ladas	31.80	1	
	6	Prez's Son	15.20	2	

Lib	6	Soda Pop	33.60	1 2 3
AP	2	The Thing to Do	29.80	1 2
	3	*(Suave Host	18.40	1
		(Oil Lease	2nd 8-1	1 2

Perfecta 116.20

July 16

Del	2	More Sail	42.80	1 2	
	4	Royal John	22.60	1	
Suf	6	John Hunt	16.80		3*

July 17

Lib	6	Sandy Reject	14.00	1 2 3
Rkm	10	Big M'shuba	19.60	1 2

July 18

Rkm	5	Reach Out	44.20	2
	9	Leap Year Miss	17.00	1 2
AP	5	Freeze Menow	19.80	1 2

July 19

Del	7	Mr. Evasive	27.80	1 2
Lib	9	Happy Tom	12.20	1 2
AP	4	Cash or Carry	12.20	1 2

July 20

Aqu	2	Deutschmark	14.40	1 2
Mth	6	Inborn	24.20	1 2 3

July 21

Aqu	2	Exe III	16.80	1 2 3
Mth	5	Amber Kitten	13.20	3
Del	1	Sec	42.20	2 3
	3	No No Fool	80.00	1 2
Lib	1	Revus	17.80	1 2 3
	4	Lady Carmella	15.60	1 2
Rkm	9	Raven's Nova	30.80	1 2

July 22

Mth	2	Champagne Carol	16.80	1 2 3	
Lib	2	Suspicious Manner	18.20	1 2 3	
Rkm	8	Kiss and Run	38.60	2 3	
AP	2	Sorta Like	15.20	1 2	

July 23

Del	9	Purple Grapes	18.80	1	

July 24

Mth	1	Bowl Pro	55.00	1	
	4	Bright and Breezy	16.20	2 3	
Del	6	Belle Princess	21.40	3*	
	8	Get Araction	37.60	1	
Lib	6	Sound Investment	12.20	3	

July 25

AP	2	Spring Patrol	13.20	1 2	
	3	Lady Ali	20.20	1	

July 26

Aqu	6	Emotional Scene	27.60	3	
Del	8	Bated Cloud	34.40	2	
Lib	4	Repayment	17.00	1 2 3	
	7	Bosun's Moud	23.40	3	
	8	Penny Rooker	16.40	1 2	
Rkm	6	Caliburn Prince	12.80	3*	
	9	Double Quill	17.60	1	
AP	1	Dollar Stride	83.80	1 2	
	5	Rising Breeze	40.80	1	

July 27

Lib	1	Sea Bouquet	15.00	1 2	
	4	Manalapan Queen	17.60	1 2 3	

July 28

Aqu	8	Scungagad	29.40	2	

Mth	9	Sailor George	25.20			3
Del	8	Our Papoose	23.40		2	
	9	Indigo Morn	34.20	1	2	
Rkm	2	Proficiency	14.20	1	2	

July 29

Lib	9	Kaloha Hill	15.80			3
AP	4	Helio Flight	14.20	1	2	

July 30

Del	9	Paddy Mick	41.20	1	2	

July 31

Sar	1	Spread the Word	12.60	1		
	5	North Flight	42.40	1		
Mth	3	Evas Bandido	30.40	1		
Del	4	Pilsner	15.20	1		
	7	Lothian Prince	26.80	1	2	3
	9	Wynnetime	12.60	1	2	3
Rkm	7	Prince Solomon	15.20	1	2	
AP	1	Iron Witness	14.20	1	2	

August 1

Sar	1	Stellar Event	26.40	1		
	8	Wakefield Miss	13.60	1	2	3
Mth	4	Trunnion	12.40	1	2	3
Rkm	6	Hy Miles	18.40	1	2	3
AP	2	Judge Delta	22.00	1	2	
	6	Big Brown	14.20	1	2	

August 2

Sar	4	Mistagrandslam	15.20	1	2	
Rkm	1	Nelson J.	32.60			3
AP	9	Shoot Little Luke	12.60			3

August 3

Mth	2	Kayrang	16.40	1	2	
	5	Bold Place	24.60	1	2	
	9	Last Minute Man	21.00			3

Del	7	Sherbrooke	31.40	1 2 3
Lib	1	Easy Finance	16.80	1 2 3
Rkm	8	Forgive Divine	41.20	1
AP	2	Behave Now	16.40	1 2

August 4

Sar	4	Princesa Rafina	22.80	1 2
	9	Pilgrim's Progress	17.80	1 2 3
Del	9	Ingrained Lassie	20.60	1 2
Lib	7	Great Esteem	23.80	1 2 3
Rkm	9	Sharp B.	17.40	1 2
AP	5	Oil Lease	18.60	1 2

August 5

Sar	1	Dr. Ralph Robbins	39.60	1 2 3
Del	9	Axton	24.00	1 2 3
Lib	2	Fleet Crown	16.00	1 2 3
	9	Bank Check	16.80	3*
Rkm	6	King of Rain	68.20	1 2

August 7

Sar	3	Delta Lady	15.00	1 2 3
Del	2	Mr. Dum Dum	52.60	1 2 3
AP	2	Double Day	20.20	1 2

August 8

Mth	1	Conquering Pet	26.80	1 2 3
Rkm	9	Best Jet	13.80	1 2
AP	3	Hi Ren	16.20	2 3

August 9

Sar	2	Tin Goose	59.80	1
Mth	3	Paper Peddler	22.00	1
Lib	1	Dumpy Kid	17.20	1 2 3
Rkm	4	Vodika	17.40	1

August 10

| Del | 7 | Classic Tudor | 18.40 | 1 |
| Lib | 5 | Our Scene | 12.20 | 1 2 3 |

August 11

Sar	1	Chartered Course	25.00	1 2 3
	8	Chrisaway	106.60	3
Mth	2	Fisherman's Wake	16.00	1 2 3
Lib	7	Braine Lechateau	14.00	1 2

August 12

Mth	9	Itta Bena	19.60	1 2
Lib	1	Tonwood (12-1)	10.80^T	1 2

August 13

De¹.	10	Light Fleet	25.80	1 2 3

August 14

Sar	8	Joy Rider	14.40	1
	9	Wild Amber	21.20	1
Lib	3	Gallant Memory	18.00	1
Rkm	9	Pilot Knob	15.80	1 2
LD	7	Truly Impressive	29.20	1 2 3
	9	Dude's Peri	17.80	1 2 3

August 15

Rkm	6	Bold Caesar	16.40	1 2

August 16

Sar	2	Roman Decision	12.80	1 2
	8	Out of School	15.00	1 2
Mth	4	Jolly Husky	29.60	3
	5	Lady Mickey	21.80	1 2
LD	8	Eda's Brandy	34.60	3
AP	8	Proven Flight	28.60	1 2

August 17

Mth	6	Size Her Up	22.40	1 2
Lib	3	Reason to Sing	38.80	1 2
Rkm	3	Solitary Man	19.20	1 2 3
	8	Flute Boy	18.00	1 2

AP	7	Madam Moody	37.80	3*
	8	Hep	19.40	2 3

August 18

Mth	3	Suburban Squire	12.80	1 2
LD	7	No Night	25.80	3
AP	1	Little Fooler	54.60	3*
	5	Stage Judge	19.40	1 2
	8	Polar Miss	16.20	2

August 19

Mth	2	Sailor's Angel	18.00	3
Lib	7	Gun Wadding	24.00	1 2
	9	Bank Check	64.80	1 2 3
AP	7	Wing Out	18.60	1
	9	Roman Leader	19.40	1 2 3

August 22

Lib	4	Samco	18.40	1 2 3
AP	7	Spring To It	46.00	1

August 23

Sar	6	Mongo's Image	17.00	1 2 3
Lib	2	Torrunner	32.00	2 3

August 24

Sar	3	Schnappy	28.20	1 2
	5	Bold Nix	51.00	3
Atl	9	Dacquare	21.80	1 2
Lib	2	Red Fog	15.20	1 2 3
LD	1	Pointress	68.20	1 2 3
	3	Tax Loss	23.00	3*
	7	Ester's Fortune	19.60	1 2 3
AP	3	Golden Strings	38.60	1 2 3

August 25

Lib	4	Midnite Run	20.60	1 2

LD	4	Toms Ruler	15.80			3
AP	4	Dream to Order	28.80			3*
	9	Li'l Sharp Nail	41.60		2	

August 26

Sar	6	Earls Erma	31.20	1	2	
Atl	5	Gillingham	27.00	1	2	
	7	Code of Honor	22.20	1	2	
Lib	6	Castle Flower	15.80	1	2	
Rkm	1	Miss Cement	23.60	1	2	3
	5	Cantilever	12.20			3
	5	Maison de Ville	22.60	1	2	
LD	5	First Crack	18.60	1	2	
AP	1	Gliding Stride	13.60	1	2	3
	4	Playhoko	12.00		2	3

August 28

Bel	6	Fearless Gal	22.20	1		
	7	Chou Croute	21.60	1	2	
LD	6	Rasputin II	12.80	1		

August 29

Bel	3	Tar Bright	23.40	1	2	
Atl	7	Richa Judge	12.20	1		
Rkm	5	Spiritis	77.00	1		
Spt	5	Royal Pine	15.60	1	2	
	9	Duty	26.20	1	2	

August 30

Atl	8	Tu Nat (entry)	16.20	1	2	3
LD	1	Psychopath	15.20	1	2	3
	9	Sultans Favor	17.00	1	2	
Spt	3	King David Dee	17.20	1	2	

August 31

Bel	2	Sara S.	12.20	1		
	8	Mortally	18.80	1	2	
Atl	4	Mrs. Shenker	42.60	1	2	
Rkm	8	Ta Co Pet	22.20	1	2	

Sep. 1

Atl	2	Ten Paces	30.80	1 2
	7	No Variance	24.00	2
LD	2	Stop the Clock	29.40	3

Sep. 2

Atl	3	Middle Date	16.60	1 2
LD	1	Long Call	34.00	1 2
	2	Babulane	15.40	1 2

Daily double 350.20

| | 3 | Sylvan Lake | 13.80 | 3* |

Sep. 4

Rkm	5A	Kentucky Flipper	32.00	2 3
	9A	Flute Boy	33.80	1 2 3
LD	7	That's Why	14.20	1 2 3
	8	Off Easy (12-1)	13.00^T	1 2 3

Sep. 5

Bel	5	Coraggioso	81.00	1
	8	Lucky Pants	14.80	1 2
Spt	6	Our Bold Bid	22.40	1 2

Sep. 6

| Atl | 4 | Fairy Boots | 177.00 | 1 2 |

Sep. 8

Rkm	2	Fierce Devotion	71.60	1 2
LD	6	Warring Lady	19.00	3
	8	Noble Hostess	17.40	2
	9	Lucky Leprechaun	27.20	1

Sep. 9

Bel	5	Rockville	12.80	2 3
Rkm	7	Knock Card	22.60	1 2 3
	8	Adaptive Ace	62.40	1 2 3
Spt	4	Joyous Judge	13.00	1 2
	7	Starsweet	27.60	2 3

Sep. 11

Bel	5	Witness Stand	13.60		3
Atl	6	Star Edition	12.80	1 2	3
	8	Love Not	15.40	1 2	
Rkm	2	Gato Grande (5-1)	6.00^T	1 2	3

Sep. 12

Bel	4	Backwoods	19.00	1 2	3
Atl	1	Village Notion	12.60	1 2	3
	2	Smart Lad	22.80	1 2	
Daily double 277.20					
	8	Corporation	14.20	1	
Rkm	2	Sentient	77.60	1 2	
Spt	1	Oxford Ali	31.20	1 2	3

Sep. 13

Atl	2	Windy Zone	28.80	1 2	
	8	Getajetholme	14.80	1 2	

Sep. 14

Atl	1	Ev's Pride	18.20	1 2	
	4	Carry My Hope	13.40	2	3
	6	Pet Rhythm	23.20	1 2	3
	9	Red and Ready	16.20		3*
LD	8	Royal Condi	18.20	1 2	
Spt	2	Nalled	20.00	1 2	3
	6	Tammy Tam	15.20	1	
	9	Oak	13.40	1 2	3

Sep. 15

Rkm	8	Happy Event	13.80	1

Sep. 16

Atl	8	Acclimatization	26.60	1 2	
Rkm	9	Step Gently	17.60	1 2	
LD	1	Big Sam D.	25.00	1 2	3
	9	Contos	14.80		3

Sep. 18

| Rkm | 6 | Fenity's Rule | 20.20 | 1 2 |
| | 7 | Bright Adversary | 67.00 | 1 2 3 |

Sep. 19

Bel	1	Wopeedah	18.40	2
	2	Misty Cat	58.00	1 2
Daily double 302.20				
	5	Shunned	19.60	1
	8	Check List	21.60	1 2 3

Sep. 20

Bel	1	Exe III	13.00	2
	7	Canonero II	13.00	1 2
Atl	6	Sneakin' Deacon	62.80	1 2
Rkm	5	Persian Castle	19.80	1 2 3
LD	2	Devil's Reject	42.40	1 2
	3	Accord the Queen	20.80	1 2 3
Spt	4	Merry Market	25.40	1 2 3

Sep. 21

Bel	3	Opinionation	55.80	1 2
	9	Windato	30.80	1 2
Rkm	7	Activism	55.00	2
LD	3	World O Fun	26.20	3
	9	Glorious Combat	23.80	1 2 3

Sep. 22

Bel	4	Song Title	17.80	1
	5	Cup Bearer	46.00	2
Rkm	1	Coriente	24.00	1 2 3
Spt	9	Duke's Bo	30.20	1 2 3

Sep. 23

| LD | 9 | Aden G. | 17.20 | 3 |

Sep. 25

Rkm	2	Stack Pack	31.40	1 2 3
LD	3	Run Lampy	12.00	1 2 3
Spt	5	Pink Mountain	14.80	1

Sep. 26

Atl	4	Village Notion	24.20	1 2 3
Spt	7	Kimble Jr.	12.60	2 3
	8	Princess Prairie	59.00	1 2 3

Sep. 27

Bel	9	Caliber	12.40	1 2
Atl	7	Rosaryville	20.80	1 2
LD	3	Maverick Belle	17.60	1

Sep. 28

Bel	1	Wearin o the Green	30.60	1
	7	Society Column	21.20	1 2
LD	1	Pawn	187.60	1 2 3
Spt	5	Makin Tracks	16.20	1 2 3
	8	Pat R.	68.00	3*

Sep. 29

Bel	2	Spear (field)	16.80	3*
	5	Young Lady	16.60	1
Atl	8	Mongo's Image	54.40	1 2
Rkm	6	Pineland	36.40	1

Sep. 30

Bel	1	Gustavus Adolphus	21.00	1 2
Rkm	7	Ky. Hard Boot	14.40	3*
	10	Wandering Tattler	17.60	1 2
Spt	9	Sylvan Head	41.40	1 2

Oct. 2

Bel	9	Delver	14.60	1 2
Lrl	3	C. C.'s Birthday	38.80	1

| Rkm | 4 | Paradisia (entry) | 15.80 | 1 2 3 |
| LD | 5 | Calcasieu Pass | 20.00 | 3* |

Oct. 3

Atl	3	Enjagee	24.40	3*
	9	We're Ahome	14.40	1 2 3
Lrl	7	Imapuncher	12.40	1
Rkm	8	Persian Warrior	14.20	1 2

Oct. 4

| Atl | 7 | Fun Man | 86.80 | 3 |
| LD | 2 | Our Alvin | 22.20 | 1 2 |

Oct. 5

Bel	8	Appear	13.00	1 2
LD	2	Carnival Carol	38.40	1 2 3
Spt	9	His Cookin	51.60	1 2

Oct. 6

| Bel | 9 | Dr. Brawner | 15.60 | 3 |

Oct. 7

| Rkm | 3 | Another Gift | 26.60 | 3 |

Oct. 9

Atl	1	Mrs. Lot	33.80	3
	4	Fated	12.20	1 2
Lrl	3	Restless Urge	13.60	1 2

Oct. 10

Bel	5	Little Rap	13.80	1
Atl	4	Paleface	28.80	1
Rkm	1	Colliding	41.40	1 2 3
	2	Northern Song	43.40	3

Daily double 849.20

| | 5 | Sentient | 13.60 | 1 2 3 |
| Spt | 1 | Last Noble | 32.00 | 3 |

Spt	2	Wool Me	22.00	1 2 3

Daily double 250.60

	5	Nowata	21.80	1 2

Oct. 11

Bel	2	Infer	17.60	1
	3	Conference Table	16.80	1 2 3
	6	Flying Fur	29.20	1 2
Rkm	1	Fleet Ascot	19.60	2 3
Spt	3	Free Forever	21.40	1 2

Oct. 12

Atl	9	Scenic Sky	81.20	1 2
Rkm	2	Double Sybil	38.20	3*
LD	4	Little Squire	34.40	1

Oct. 13

Rkm	2	With a Passion	31.40	3*
	7	Cherry Hill Pro	18.00	1 2 3
LD	5	James Stuart	13.60	1 2 3

Oct. 14

Bel	1	Silver Shield	28.00	3*
	5	Fernande	29.60	1 2
Atl	9	Old Scotch	15.20	3
Lrl	1	Beats A Blank	28.20	2 3
LD	2	Flying Jorayme	35.00	1 2 3
	5	Contos	22.20	1 2
	7	Linden Creek	20.20	1 2 3
	9	Dad Daw	21.80	1 2

Oct. 15

Suf	1	Helioroad	78.00	1 2 3

Oct. 16

Aqu	4	Double Rye	13.40	1
Lrl	1	Evil Tudor	18.00	1 2
Suf	3	Paradisia	70.00	3*
LD	5	Middle Fury	21.40	1 2

Oct. 18

Lrl	6	Nakula	24.00	1 2
	9	Prince Joker	14.80	1 2
Spt	1	Just Like Uptown	30.80	1

Oct. 19

Aqu	9	Flying Crimson	20.80	1
Lrl	7	Flashing Socks	18.80	1 2 3
Suf	6	Waysan	57.60	3*
LD	9	Follow Us	21.40	2 3

Oct. 20

Suf	2	Neo Sea	14.80	1 2
Spt	1	Greeks Image	15.20	1
	2	Escon	55.80	1 2 3

Daily double 349.00

Oct. 21

Aqu	3	Amerikingdom	18.40	1 2
	4	Little On	15.00	1 2 3
	8	Rooney's Shield	12.40	1 2
GS	7	Pat Henry	14.80	1 2
Suf	2	Polly Ladd	17.00	2 3
	4	Brainwashed	12.20	1 2 3
Spt	5	Fever Mark	82.00	2 3

Oct. 23

Aqu	3	Sweet Balcony	18.20	3*
GS	9	Hillys Joe	22.00	1 2
Lrl	2	Bard of Cornwall	15.00	1 2
	9	Hang In There	15.00	2 3
Suf	9	Prize Miss	36.60	1
LD	6	Wednesday Off	21.60	3*
	14	Sultans Favor	13.40	1 2
Spt	4	Late Admiral	27.60	2 3

Oct. 24

| Aqu | 9 | Colonel Jerry | 22.80 | 1 2 |

Spt	3	Musical Tee	140.20	3*
	8	Superior Hands	16.20	1 2

Oct. 25

GS	2	Nationalist	19.60	1 2 3
	8	Candid Catherine	16.80	1
Suf	8	Dream Spot	12.20	1 2 3
Spt	1	Flitter Klu	12.40	1 2 3

Oct. 26

Aqu	7	New Tune	21.60	1 2 3
LD	7	Royal Condi	37.40	1 2
Spt	1	Lebanese Doctor	28.00	3

Oct. 28

GS	2	Valtona	13.60	1 2
	7	Good John	22.20	1 2
Lrl	4	Suspended	22.40	1 2
LD	1	Oil Rullah	13.80	1 2 3
Spt	7	Glory Run	28.60	1

Oct. 29

Suf	8	Risky Alibhai	21.00	1 2 3

Oct. 30

Aqu	1	Tropical Sunset	49.00	2 3
	8	Supper Show	46.00	3
GS	4	Gallant Memory	53.00	1 2
Lrl	4	I Didn't	13.40	1 2 3
Suf	2	Legislation	13.00	1 2
LD	1	Selected Set	26.00	1 2 3

Oct. 31

GS	1	Miss Imagination	17.00	1 2
	9	Chatty Catty	16.00	1 2
Spt	6	Flying Cupid	23.20	2

Nov. 1

GS	1	Rapid Fashion	33.20	1 2 3

GS	4	Run Columbia	14.40		2 3
Suf	3	Asia Cee (13-1)	13.60^T		2 3
Spt	5	Gentle Giant	28.60	1	
	7	Red Cedar	24.20	1 2	

Nov. 2

GS	4	Indifference	12.20	1	
	7	Caprice Miss	20.80	1 2	
	8	Jump Seat	16.40	1 2	
Lrl	4	Dr. George M.	22.60	1 2 3	
Suf	1	Stylist Louie	19.00	2	
Spt	1	Tempermental Tom	23.00	3	
	7	Freeze Menow	25.40	1 2 3	

Nov. 3

Aqu	2	Cumbre Velo	19.20	1	
GS	5	Tudor Rascal	12.00		3
	6	Escaped	14.60		3*
	8	Barnabas	13.40		3
Suf	5	Douvrendelle	50.20		3*
	8	Passing On	23.80	1 2 3	
LD	2	Billy Boy	23.60	1	
Spt	1	Brown Cup	28.60		3

Nov. 4

Aqu	7	Grafitti	20.80	1	
GS	4	Pride of the Corps	12.20	1 2	

Nov. 5

Suf	4	Beau Star	14.60	2	

Nov. 6

Aqu	1	Stray Shell	30.80	1 2	
	4	Lover's Tryst	13.20	1	
Lrl	2	Ski Girl	15.20	1 2	
	5	Bold David	18.00		3*
LD	5	Tourist Trip	21.40	1 2	

Nov. 7

Aqu	1	Snappy John (field)	18.40		3

Aqu	4	Prized Memory	19.40	1 2 3
LD	2	Macajo	37.60	2
Spt	1	Triboletion	24.40	1

Nov. 8

Aqu	7	Decimator	44.00	1
Suf	1	My Son Don	41.00	2 3
	2	Spinover	92.20	1 2
Daily double 655.00				
Spt	8	Tammy Tam	39.20	1 2 3

Nov. 9

| Aqu | 6 | Doc Gibson | 17.20 | 1 2 3 |
| Suf | 7 | Siklara | 17.00 | 1 2 3 |

Nov. 10

GS	7	Baqueta	24.40	1
Lrl	9	Mroning Charger	42.40	3
Spt	8	Cactus Will	66.20	1 2 3

Nov. 13

| LD | 2 | Long Range | 28.80 | 1 |
| Spt | 4 | Lil Terry | 12.20 | 2 |

Nov. 14

| GS | 7 | Go Go Pago | 17.40 | 1 2 |
| Lrl | 4 | Radu | 15.20 | 1 2 |

Nov. 15

GS	3	Papa Gaudio	18.80	1 2
	9	Fall Rush	29.20	1 2
Suf	3	Bold Esteem	38.60	1 2
Spt	7	Amiles Duke	14.20	3*

Nov. 16

Aqu	5	Kup Runneth	49.20	1 2
Suf	4	Late for School	15.00	2
	5	Win Trip	26.00	1 2 3

LD	3	Autumn Charger	20.20	1 2 3
	5	Count Swerve	73.00	1 2
	6	Running Mont	28.00	1 2 3
Spt	5	Sea Toy	14.00	1 2

Nov. 17

Aqu	1	Double Message	21.60		3
	5	Tropical Heat	59.80		2
GS	1	Summer Jane	34.20	1 2
Suf	6	Sentient	13.20	1 2
	7	Poppa Grande	19.00	1
Spt	2	Milagro's Wander	14.20		3
	4	Jet Delivery	20.40	1 2
	5	Marine Flyer	12.80	1

Nov. 18

GS	7	Glider Boy	25.60	1
LD	2	Deep Pool	42.60	1 2 3
	8	Nobody Cares	37.80		3
Spt	9	Barataria Pass	12.20	1 2

Nov. 19

Suf	1	Sky Fort	49.80	1 2
	5	Pink Carnation	17.80	1
	8	My Secret Love	12.20	1 2

Nov. 20

Lrl	2	Alice's Idol	13.00		3
Suf	2	Le Beau Fols	23.60	1
Crc	8	Ellies Nashua	19.20		3

Nov. 21

Aqu	8	Rum Raisin	13.60	1 2
Lrl	4	Talamanca	17.40	1 2

Nov. 22

Aqu	8	Viborg	12.60		2
Lrl	2	Noor Side	20.80	1
Crc	1	Girl Returns	24.40	1 2

Nov. 23

Aqu	4	Tommy P.	17.80	1	2	
	5	Rooney's Shield	15.80	1	2	3
FG	5	Beaverville	29.40	1	2	

Nov. 25

Lib	1	Big Build Up	19.00	1		
Lrl	7	Coppabarb	37.40	1		
FG	1	Bold Relations	15.60	1		

Nov. 27

Lib	7	Farmer George	26.00	1	2	
Suf	3	Com Perry	34.00	1	2	
	7	Big Bob L.	25.00	1	2	3
Crc	5	Vive Le Ruler	19.40	1	2	
FG	6	Middle Roman	38.60	1	2	

Nov. 29

Lib	8	Chateauvira	29.60	1	2	
Suf	3	Top Miss	186.20	1	2	
	6	Methuselah	31.40	1	2	3
Crc	3	Abdul Aziz	72.60	1	2	

Nov. 30

Lib	4	Rose Glow	39.20			3
Lrl	3	Sir Jig	15.60	1	2	
	5	Marvin's Windy	41.00		2	
Crc	5	Oh Dee	123.20			3*
	9	Holmestretch	22.60	1	2	
	10	Locksmith	22.20	1	2	
FG	4	Furyman	12.80	1	2	3

Dec. 1

Suf	7	Sebrina Lane	26.40			3
	9	Styrullah	18.40	1	2	
Crc	6	Sister C.	14.00			3
	10	Murray G.	19.40	1	2	
FG	7	All Flags Flying	19.00	1		

Dec. 2

Aqu	8	Eager Exchange	28.00	1 2	
Lib	7	Lost Idol	16.20	1 2 3	
	9	Alject	47.60	1 2	
Lrl	8	Amber Hawk	21.00	1 2	
Suf	8	John Hunt	13.20	1 2 3	
Crc	2	Cold Draft	39.00		3*
	4	Tropical Flirt	23.40	1 2 3	
	7	Duke Of Whitman	41.20	1 2	
	10	Smiley Miley	12.00	1	
FG	5	Mr. Nerida	16.20	1	
	10	Blue Chippee	29.80		3*

Dec. 3

Suf	1	Smiley Lou	13.00	1 2
	5	Alishay	24.60	1 2 3

Dec. 4

Aqu	6	Harberer	29.00		3*
Lrl	6	Safety Blitz	17.00	1 2 3	
Crc	3	King Rolf	13.60	1	
LD	7	So Brave	53.40	1 2 3	
	9	Trudys Duty	22.20	1	

Dec. 5

Aqu	8	Domineer III	19.60	1 2 3		
Crc	6	King of Ironwood	20.60			3
	8	Autumn's End	14.60		2	

Dec. 6

Lrl	4	Landing Gray	17.60	1
Crc	9	Raise a Dancer	14.80	1 2

Dec. 7

Lib	4	Weigh Anchor	22.20	1 2 3
Lrl	7	Crimson Tigre	23.40	1 2 3
Crc	5	Best Direction	12.60	1 2
LD	2	Victory Note	17.00	1

| LD | 4 | Sandra B Good | 46.00 | 1 2 3 |
| FG | 2 | Sport Family | 39.60 | 1 |

Dec. 8

| LD | 7 | Jeepose | 31.60 | 1 2 |

Dec. 9

Aqu	6	Proven Tune	18.00	1 2
Lib	6	Ace Star	18.80	1
LD	1	Free Boy	12.20	3
	6	Willow Star	17.20	1
FG	3	Mack To Market	14.40	1 2
	10	Bosun's Girl	19.60	3

Dec. 11

Lrl	1	Ebony Sea	15.80	2
	8	Far Fetched	54.20	1 2 3
Lib	8	Chance Miltie	21.40	1
Crc	4	Funbun Star	18.60	1 2
LD	1	Mini Me	17.40	1
	6	Flying Jorayme	12.60	1 2
FG	1	La Neige	14.20	1

Dec. 12

| Lib | 3 | Tamed | 27.40 | 1 2 |

Dec. 13

Aqu	1	Poly Joy	15.00	1
	6	Tudor Crest	34.20	1 2 3
Lrl	9	Cash Blue	12.40	1 2
Lib	7	Social Endeavour	29.00	1 2 3
Crc	9	Aye Aye Jay	20.80	1 2
LD	3	Fasaru	66.40	2
FG	3	Pilot's Pinsetter	12.60	1

Dec. 14

Aqu	6	A Penny Saved	16.40	3*
Lib	4	Terry's Start	34.80	1 2 3
	5	The Redeemer	16.00	2
Crc	9	Nose For Money	31.00	2

Dec. 15

Aqu	4	Imperial Majesty	19.00	1 2 3
	9	Honey Galore	31.00	1 2 3
Lrl	1	Lead All	16.40	1
Lib	2	Crim Potatoes	17.40	1
	9	Awake Sue	23.60	1 2 3
FG	1	Won't Dance	18.60	1 2

Dec. 16

Aqu	1	Eagles Spring	33.00	2 3
	8	Ghost Train	29.00	3
Lib	7	Second Counter	14.80	1 2 3

Dec. 18

Crc	6	Frustrate	13.20	1

Dec. 19

Crc	7	Let Em Boil	16.20	2
	8	Turf Mac	46.20	1 2

Dec. 20

Lrl	1	Barnesville Belle	145.20	2
Crc	5	Noble Duel	20.00	1 2
	6	J A King Jr.	73.80	1 2
LD	2	Eartha Twirl	13.60	2
	4	Tax Talk	34.20	1 2 3
FG	6	Crack the Whip	23.80	1

Dec. 21

Lib	6	Peter G.	30.80	3*
Crc	6	Trigger Happy	84.00	1 2
	7	Urbanow	12.20	1
FG	8	Big Dot	12.60	1 2

Dec. 22

Lib	9	Elva's Story	18.00	1
Crc	5	Gal Of The Islands	18.20	1
FG	7	Red Swap	14.40	1
	10	Pass Receiver	27.00	3

Dec. 24

				1	2	3
FG	10	Making Noise	15.60			3

Dec. 25

				1	2	3
Crc	5	Sensitive Key	64.40		2	
	6	Overide	47.40			3

Dec. 26

				1	2	3
Lrl	1	Villa Verde	14.00	1		
Lib	1	Gilgal	22.20	1	2	
LD	7	Five Grand	13.20			3
FG	2	Misty Claim	42.80	1	2	
	9	Prince Terrell	17.40	1		
SA	6	Shawnex	20.20	1	2	

Dec. 27

				1	2	3
Crc	2	Santa Nora	27.00	1		
	4	Castleaire	41.20		2	

Dec. 28

				1	2	3
Lrl	1	Belles Arrohead	26.60		2	
LD	2	Spanish Tango	43.80	1	2	
	4	Shad Rig	14.40	1		
	8	King Harvest	22.60	1	2	
SA	7	Prince o' Pace	37.60	1	2	

Dec. 29

				1	2	3
Lib	9	Ah Netta	20.20	1	2	
LD	4	Gemagain	18.20	1		
	8	Helen Ross	22.00	1	2	
FG	1	Gray Charm	17.20		2	3
SA	3	Scottina B.	17.20	1		

Dec. 30

				1	2	3
Lib	4	Hindiya	16.60	1	2	3
LD	9	Ema Poochie	17.60	1	2	3

Dec. 31

Suf	9	Minstrel Clown	12.40	1 2
FG	5	Trader Nick	28.80	1
	7	Rowbeaumarl	25.00	2 3

Appendix 2

SOME OUTER-CALL PERFORMANCE
RATING WINNERS

Jan. 1

Trp	7	Beef Baron	54.80	1 2	

Jan. 3

Trp	6	Westgate Mall	31.80	1	
	10	Hardy Hugh	20.60	1 2 3	

Jan. 4

Lib	6	Happy Tom	52.80	1	
FG	1	#Molloqua	43.80	1 2	
	5	#American Lass	20.80	1 2	

Jan. 8

Nar	5	Brother Emmanuel	39.80	1 2 3	

Jan. 10

Trp	6	Tropical Pilot	25.40	1	

Jan. 15

Bow	6	Night Patrol	28.20	1 2	
FG	2	Plaza Beau	22.60	1 2	

Jan. 17

Bow	7	Our Wallflower	56.60	1	

149

		Jan. 19		
Lib	4	#Ft. King	49.20	1 2
		Jan. 22		
FG	7	John Jet	26.20	1
SA	1	King's Delegate	36.40	1 2 3
	6	#Aggressively	24.80	1 2
		Jan. 29		
GP	9	Close Decision	53.60	2
		Jan. 31		
Bow	6	#Stage Trust (entry)	24.60	1 2 3
FG	6	#Taul Hill	24.80	1 2 3
		Feb. 2		
SA	1	Chocolate Tree	28.60	1 2 3
		Feb. 3		
Lib	5	#Positive Pete	88.20	1 2 3
GP	10	Bobs B Bees	24.80	2 3
		Feb. 4		
Lib	4	Dressy Lad	52.80	1 2 3
		Feb. 10		
SA	5	#Calgary Miss	44.40	1 2
		Feb. 15		
Bow	7	Heavenly Robes	28.60	1 2
		Feb. 16		
GP	4	Silver Mark II	24.80	1 2

		Feb. 17		
Bow	3	Mr. Judex	47.80	1

		Feb. 23		
Bow	2	Tul Echo	36.20	1 2

		Feb. 25		
Nar	1	Bill Jr.	48.00	1 2 3

		Feb. 28		
FG	7	Reechlight	39.80	1 2 3

		March 4		
Hia	4	Ruff King Bergeruk	28.80	1 2
Nar	1	Ear Ring	26.20	

		March 6		
Nar	5	Disatate	23.20	1 2

		March 8		
Nar	2	All Sadair	22.40	3

		March 9		
Hia	7	Shambo Lain	20.40	3

		March 11		
Hia	2	Topi	26.80	1 2

Daily double $550.60. (Picadilly Red, picked by both Equal Call and Outer Call Rating Plans, won the first race, paying $24.60.)

		March 15		
Hia	6	Lin-D Star	20.80	1
SA	8	Tin-Tin II.	34.80	1 2

		March 17		
FG	10	Miss Matey	43.40	1 2
		March 18		
Hia	1	#Brave Gypsy	62.00	1 2
		March 22		
Suf	5	Escape Me Never	30.80	1
		March 23		
FG	2	Toeless Tom	20.40	
		March 25		
Nar	7	Just Could	31.20	1 2

Appendix 3

SOME TOP-TWO-RATING PRICE FACTOR WINNERS

		Oct. 2		
Atl	8	Slady Castle	31.60	1 2

		Oct. 5		
Spt	1	Polar Dance	28.60	1 2

		Oct. 6		
Rkm	1	May Ban	37.00	1 2 3

		Oct. 7		
Atl	1	Delica Tessie	50.00	1 2

		Oct. 21		
LD	1	Blazing Miss	26.40	1 2

		Oct. 24		
Aqu	2	Sinamar	149.40	1 2

		Oct. 30		
GS	9	Roji	21.60	1 2
Lrl	1	Summer Planning	21.00	1 2

		Nov. 1		
Spt	8	Yalou	125.20	1 2

Nov. 4

| GS | 2 | Tootieboy | 45.40 | 1 |
| | 9 | Our Hope's Caper | 102.80 | 1 2 |

Nov. 8

| Suf | 5 | Kawachi | 27.80 | 1 2 |

Nov. 9

| Aqu | 1 | Marquis de Sade | 31.80 | 1 |
| Lrl | 4 | Third Law | 83.20 | 1 2 |

Nov. 11

| Suf | 1 | Nick Saponara | 77.20 | 1 |

Nov. 15

Lrl	4	Crimson Tigre	25.40	1
Spt	4	Shirley P.	30.80	1 2
	9	Analyst	31.60	1 2 3

Nov. 16

| Suf | 6 | King Orange | 56.00 | 1 2 |

Nov. 20

| Crc | 2 | Jestajoy | 45.00 | 1 2 |

Nov. 23

| LD | 4 | Cover Crop | 41.60 | 1 2 |

Nov. 27

| Aqu | 3 | D. P. Run Off | 65.20 | 1 2 |

Nov. 29

| Lrl | 1 | Auntie Joan | 59.00 | 1 2 3 |

		Nov. 30		
Lib	5	Sunset Drums	74.40	1 2
		Dec. 1		
Lrl	9	Dasha Bitters	30.20	1 2
		Dec. 12		
Aqu	8	Bold Skipper	50.00	1 2
		Dec. 14		
Lrl	5	Piney Run	48.20	1
		Dec. 15		
Aqu	6	Bridget O'Brick	28.80	1 2 3
Lib	4	Decorativo	38.00	1 2
		Dec. 20		
Lib	2	Monarchs Joy	25.80	1
		Dec. 21		
FG	7	Takes Two Hands	81.60	1 2
		Dec. 27		
LD	3	Oh Never	26.00	1
		Dec. 29		
Crc	5	Soft Stroke	20.20	1 2
LD	1	Lost Brook	42.20	1 2
		Dec. 30		
Lrl	2	Beats A Blank	22.00	1